Excel 2000

Further Skills

Excel 2000

Further Skills

David Weale

CONTINUUM

London · New York

Acknowledgements

The computer program Microsoft® Excel is copyrighted to Microsoft® Corporation, all rights reserved. Microsoft® Excel, Excel 2000 and Windows®98 are either registered trademarks or trademarks of Microsoft® Corporation in the United States and/or other countries.

ISBN 0-8264-5650-2

Typeset in 9/12pt Palatino by C.K.M. Typesetting, Salisbury, Wiltshire
Printed in Great Britain by CPD, Ebbw Vale

The small print

Although every care has been taken with the production of this book, the Author and the Publishers do not accept any responsibility for any failure, damage, or loss caused by following the said contents. The Author and Publisher do not take any responsibility for errors or omissions.

The Author and Publisher will not be liable to the purchaser or to any other person or legal entity with respect to any liability, loss or damage (whether direct, indirect, special, incidental or consequential) caused or alleged to be caused directly or indirectly by this book.

The book is sold as is, without any warranty of any kind, either expressed or implied, respecting the contents, including but not limited to implied warranties regarding the book's quality, performance, correctness or fitness for any particular purpose.

Contents

Preface

This book covers the advanced features within Excel; the basic features are covered in the companion book (**Excel 2000 Basic Skills**).

This book is primarily concerned with the use of Excel as a spreadsheet covering both numeric techniques and charting in depth. Using Excel as a database is not covered as this was comprehensively dealt with in **Excel 2000 Basic Skills**.

The reader should also be familiar with the techniques and concepts involved in using **Microsoft**® **Windows**®.

I hope you, the reader, will enjoy this book and learn from it.

David Weale, June 2001

Introduction

The versions of Excel

Spreadsheets have been around since the dawn of the personal computer, Microsoft® Excel was first issued in 1987 and has gone through many changes and updates. The latest version is **Excel 2000**, which is the version upon which this book is based.

Version compatibility

Excel is backwards compatible, this means that any worksheets or charts produced in previous versions should load and work within Excel 2000.

However, this compatibility relies on the necessary conversion programs being installed on your system (not all are installed by default).

Using previous versions of Excel

As Excel has become more sophisticated, the features available have expanded and some may not have been available in previous versions. This is important if you are saving a file using Excel 2000 for use in a previous version. However, the conversion programs need to have been installed.

To use **Excel 2000** files with a previous version, you need to pull down the **File** menu, select **Save As** and, after naming the file, pull down the list of **Save as type** (by clicking on the arrow to the right of the box) and select the correct version.

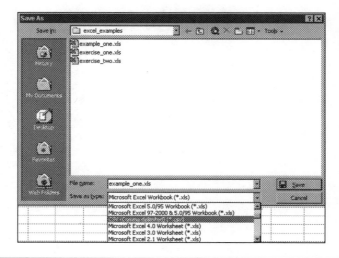

As you can see from the illustration, you are not restricted to Excel file types; you can use the Excel 2000 files with a wide variety of programs although some features of Excel may not convert successfully.

Filenames

In this version of Excel, it is not necessary to use underscores in the filename, however I have used them in the book as I like to.

File extensions

All files have an extension, which defines the type of file, for example, Excel files have *.xls* extension after the file name given by the user. The extension may not be shown (this is dependent upon the settings of your system).

Workbooks

Excel defines a file as a workbook and this convention is used in the text.

Worksheets

Cell addressing

What you will learn in this unit:

❏ The difference between relative and absolute cell addresses

❏ How to make a cell address absolute

Absolute and relative addressing

There are two types of cell address, **relative** and **absolute**.

Relative

The default method is relative addressing; this means that when you copy a formula, the cell address changes *relative* to the row or column.

Ⓐ **Activity**

❏ Begin a new file and save it as **first_example**.

❏ Please enter the following data:

	A	B	C	D	E	F	G
1		jan					
2	sales						
3	purchases						
4	profit						
5							
6		jan					
7	units sold	100	110	105	95	45	88
8	sale price per unit	£8					
9	units purchased	112	135	100	102	66	50
10	cost price per unit	£5					

AutoFill the month across the columns (**C** to **G**) for both row **1** and row **6**.

Insert a new row above row **1**.

Enter the title:

Sales Forecast

Centre this across the columns.

Save the file.

Using the worksheet you have just created, enter a formula into cell **B3** to calculate the value of the **sales** for january (*units sold* multiplied by *sale price per unit* – **B8** multiplied by **B9**).

AutoFill this across the columns (**C** to **G**).

If you view the formulas, you should see this display.

The quickest way to view the formulas is to hold down the **Ctrl** key and, while holding this down, press the **single left quotation key** (above the **tab** key).

	A	B	C	D
1				Sales Forecast
2		jan	feb	mar
3	sales	=B8*B9	=C8*C9	=D8*D9

The original formula (=**B8*B9**) changes relative to the column it is copied to (it becomes =**C8*C9** in column **C** and so on).

However, the result is incorrect as the sales value will be shown as zero for all the months apart from january.

	A	B	C	D	E	F	G
1				Sales Forecast			
2		jan	feb	mar	apr	may	jun
3	sales	£800	£0	£0	£0	£0	£0
4	purchases						
5	profit						

Absolute

An absolute cell reference (address) does not change when it is copied.

To make a cell address absolute, place a **$** sign *before* the column and/or row reference.

Use the **F4** key to make addresses absolute by highlighting the cell reference in the **formula bar** and then pressing the **F4** key.

Activity

Edit the contents of the cell **B3** to read:

=B8*$B$9

This fixes the cell address **B9** so that it remains the same when copied.

AutoFill the new formula across the columns and view the formulas.

	A	B	C	D	E	F	G
1				Sales Forecast			
2		jan	feb	mar	apr	may	jun
3	sales	£800	£880	£840	£760	£360	£704
4	purchases						
5	profit						

The figures for the sales will change from zero to the correct figures.

	A	B	C	D
1				Sales Forecast
2		jan	feb	mar
3	sales	=B8*$B$9	=C8*$B$9	=D8*$B$9
4	purchases			
5	profit			

Enter the formula for the **purchases** (*units purchased* multiplied by *cost price per unit* – **B10** multiplied by **B11**).

Make the cell reference **B11** absolute and copy the formula across the columns.

Enter a formula in cell **B5** to calculate the **profit** (*sales* minus *purchases*).

Copy this across the columns.

Name the worksheet **forecast**.

Format the worksheet professionally (use **AutoFormat** if you wish and then make any necessary changes) but ensure that the cells containing units (rows **8** and **10**) are shown as integers (whole numbers).

Use Page Setup to:

❑ Fit to one page and set to Landscape orientation.

❑ Centre the worksheet on the page.

❑ Add a header (your name) and footers (date and file name), change the fonts for these.

Save the file and preview it, it should look similar to this.

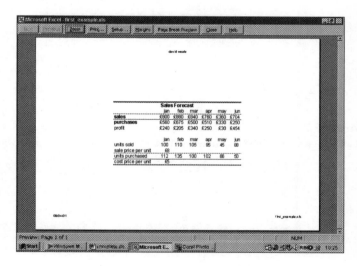

Close the file.

Functions

In this unit you will learn about:

❑ Conditional functions

❑ Using the IF statement

❑ How to predict the future using the FORECAST function.

Conditional functions

The **IF** function tests whether a condition is **true** or **false** and then what to do as a result.

The structure is:

=IF(condition, *true*, *false*)

❏ The condition is tested and **if** the condition is **true** then the **true** section of the function is carried out.

❏ If the condition is **false** (not true) then the **false** section is carried out.

Example:
=IF (it is the weekend, *stay in bed, get up and go to work*)

❏ the condition is **IF** it is the weekend

❏ If the condition is **true** then you can *stay in bed.*

❏ If the condition is **false** (it is not the weekend) then you need to *get up and go to work.*

The mathematical symbols that can be used are:

Greater than	>
Less than	<
Greater than or equal to	> =
Less than or equal to	< =

(T) The inequality sign (*greater than* or *less than*) is **always** typed before the equals sign.

(A) **Activity**

Open the workbook **first-example** and enter the following data in a new worksheet (*Sheet2*).

	A	B	C	D	E	F
1	Bonus Payments based on sales targets					
2		july	august	september	Total	Bonus
3	Sally	99	85	67		
4	Ben	45	125	41		
5	Rachael	87	67	54		
6	Total					

Calculate the totals (both row and column totals) using the **AutoSum** function and then copy the formulas to the other relevant cells in the row or column.

Name the sheet **bonuses**.

> You are told that a bonus is paid to the staff based upon the condition that if the total unit sales for the three months exceeds 250 units then a bonus of £1 per unit sold is paid, otherwise the bonus is calculated at £0.50 per unit sold.

With the cursor in cell **F3**, enter the following formula:

=IF(E3>250,E3*1,E3*0.5)

The formula tests if the unit sales are greater than 250, if this is true then the bonus is £1 for each unit sold, if the condition is false then the bonus is £0.50 per unit sold.

Copy the formula down to **F5**.

You should see the following result.

	A	B	C	D	E	F
1	Bonus Payments based on sales targets					
2		july	august	september	Total	Bonus
3	Sally	99	85	67	251	251
4	Ben	45	125	41	211	105.5
5	Rachael	87	67	54	208	104
6	Total	231	277	162	670	

The formulas should look like this.

	A	B	C	D	E	F
1	Bonus Payments based on sales					
2		july	august	september	Total	Bonus
3	Sally	99	85	67	=SUM(B3:D3)	=IF(E3>250,E3*1,E3*0.5)
4	Ben	45	125	41	=SUM(B4:D4)	=IF(E4>250,E4*1,E4*0.5)
5	Rachael	87	67	54	=SUM(B5:D5)	=IF(E5>250,E5*1,E5*0.5)
6	Total	=SUM(B3:B5)	=SUM(C3:C5)	=SUM(D3:D5)	=SUM(E3:E5)	

Format the worksheet professionally, paying attention to achieving a consistent number of decimal places within each column.

Use Page Setup to:

❑ Fit to one page and set to Landscape orientation.

❑ Centre the worksheet on the page.

❑ Add a header (your name) and footers (date and worksheet name), change the fonts for these.

The result could look like this.

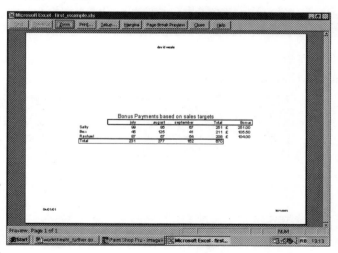

Save the file.

Ⓔ **Exercise**

❑ Enter the following data into a new worksheet (*Sheet3*), naming the worksheet **mobile phones**.

	A	B	C	D	E
1	mobile phone sales summary for 2000				
2		units sold		value	
3	month	crewkerne	yeovil	crewkerne	yeovil
4	jan	1555	999		
5	feb	1645	654		
6	mar	1231	2314		
7	apr	1784	3547		
8	may	2871	3695		
9	jun	2314	2154		
10	jul	1654	2333		
11	aug	2998	1468		
12	sep	987	2144		
13	oct	568	1699		
14	nov	1254	2145		
15	dec	3879	3256		
16	total				
17					
18	average sale price per unit	£39.99			

❏ Use **AutoSum** to calculate the total figure for the **units sold** columns.

❏ Enter a formula into **D4** to calculate the value (*units sold* multiplied by *average sale price per unit*). Do the same for cell **E4**.

❏ You will need to make part of each formula **absolute**.

❏ Copy these down (together).

❏ If they have not already been calculated, use **AutoSum** to calculate the totals for the other columns.

❏ Insert two blank rows above row **18**.

❏ Enter into cell **A18**:

Bonus

❏ Enter a formula in cell **D18** to calculate the bonus (on the following basis), copy this to **E18**.

> If the total sales value is more than £1m, a bonus of 10% of total sales value is paid, otherwise a bonus of 5% is paid.

❏ Format the worksheet to your own satisfaction.

Your results should be the same as shown below.

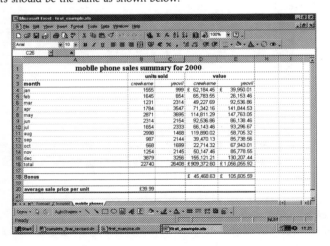

The formulas are shown below.

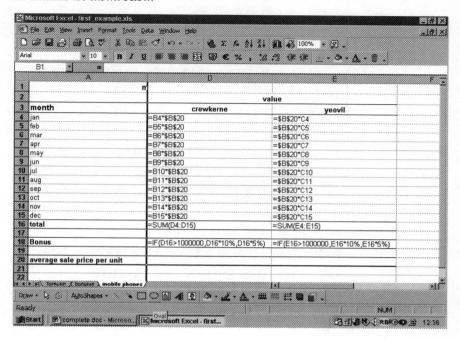

❑ Save and close the file.

The FORECAST function

Excel contains functions to enable you to estimate future results using historical data as the basis of the calculation.

 Activity

Begin a new file, saving it as **forecasting** and renaming *Sheet1* as **forecast**.

Enter the data shown in the following illustration, formatting it as desired.

	A	B	C	D	E
1		the blues bar & café			
2		sales income			
3	year	1998	1999	2000	2001
4	beer	£ 5,231	£ 5,687	£ 5,999	
5	wine	£ 1,254	£ 3,562	£ 3,326	
6	gigs	£ 1,200	£ 1,452	£ 1,587	
7	total				

Position the cursor in cell **E4** and click the **Paste Function** button on the toolbar (alternatively, pull down the **Insert** menu followed by **Function**).

Select **Statistical** from the **Function category** and then **Forecast** from the list of **Function Names**.

Enter the data shown below (using the buttons at the end of each row together with the mouse to select the data), clicking the **OK** button when finished.

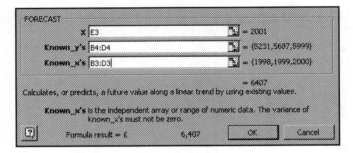

The result should predict the figure for the year **2001**.

A	B	C	D	E
1	the blues bar & café			
2	sales income			
3 year	1998	1999	2000	2001
4 beer	£ 5,231	£ 5,687	£ 5,999	£ 6,407
5 wine	£ 1,254	£ 3,562	£ 3,326	
6 gigs	£ 1,200	£ 1,452	£ 1,587	
7 total				

If you want to copy this to other cells e.g. to **E5**, you need to make use of absolute addressing to ensure that the formula copies correctly, an example of this is shown below.

> Remember that you can use the **F4** key to make addresses absolute by highlighting them in the **formula bar** and then using the **F4** key.

=FORECAST($E$3,B4:D4,$B$3:$D$3)

Make the necessary cells absolute and copy the formula down to cells **E5** and **E6**.

Finally calculate the total row and the worksheet should be similar to this.

A	B	C	D	E
1	the blues bar & café			
2	sales income			
3 year	1998	1999	2000	2001
4 beer	£5,231	£5,687	£5,999	£6,407
5 wine	£1,254	£3,562	£3,326	£4,786
6 gigs	£1,200	£1,452	£1,587	£1,800
7 total	£7,685	£10,701	£10,912	£12,993

Exercise

❏ Add a further year to the projection (**2002**) and use the **Forecast** function to predict the results for that year (remember to use only the original data (years 1998 to 2000) to predict the result.

The results should look like this.

	A	B	C	D	E	F
1	the blues bar & café					
2	sales income					
3	year	1998	1999	2000	2001	2002
4	beer	£5,231	£5,687	£5,999	**£6,407**	**£6,791**
5	wine	£1,254	£3,562	£3,326	**£4,786**	**£5,822**
6	gigs	£1,200	£1,452	£1,587	**£1,800**	**£1,994**
7	total	**£7,685**	**£10,701**	**£10,912**	**£12,993**	**£14,607**

The formulas should look like this.

	A	E	F
1		the blues bar & café	
2		sales income	
3	year	2001	2002
4	beer	=FORECAST($E$3,B4:D4,$B$3:$D$3)	=FORECAST($F$3,B4:D4,$B$3:$D$3)
5	wine	=FORECAST($E$3,B5:D5,$B$3:$D$3)	=FORECAST($F$3,B5:D5,$B$3:$D$3)
6	gigs	=FORECAST($E$3,B6:D6,$B$3:$D$3)	=FORECAST($F$3,B6:D6,$B$3:$D$3)
7	total	=SUM(E4:E6)	=SUM(F4:F6)

❏ Save and close the file.

Copying worksheets and charts

What you will learn about in this unit:

❏ How to copy worksheets to Word

❏ How to copy charts to Word

❏ Linking Word and Excel files

❏ Linking worksheets

❏ Linking workbooks

Copying worksheets to Word

It is often useful, indeed necessary, to copy worksheet data from Excel into Word, for example to include it in a report.

 ### Activity

Open a new **Word** document.

Enter the following text, format it to choice and centre it:

A report on the sales for 2000

Save it giving it the name **pasting** and then minimise the **Word** screen.

Open the Excel file **first_example** and select the worksheet named **forecast**.

Highlight all the data in the worksheet and click on the **Copy** button.

Switch to the **Word** document and position the cursor where you want the worksheet data to appear.

 Before pasting the table, it is a good idea to create space after the preceding and before the following text.

Click the **Paste** button and the data is pasted into **Word** as a table.

Click the mouse pointer within the table and pull down the **Table** menu, select **Table AutoFormat** and a suitable format.

Centre the table by selecting it and then pulling down the **Table** menu selecting **Table Properties**, followed by the **Table** tab and **Center**.

When you preview the **Word** file, it may look similar to this.

A report on the sales for 2000

Sales Forecast

	jan	feb	mar	apr	may	jun
sales	800	880	840	760	360	704
purchases	560	675	500	510	330	250
profit	240	205	340	250	30	454

	jan	feb	mar	apr	may	jun
unit sold	100	110	105	95	45	88
sale price per unit	8					
unit purchased	112	135	100	102	66	50
cost price per unit	5					

Copying charts to Word

For similar reasons, you may want to copy a chart from Excel into Word.

Activity
Switch back to **Excel**.

Create a **column chart**, on a new sheet, from the data in the worksheet **mobile phones** using the data in cells **A3** to **C15**.

Add suitable titles and format the chart as you wish.

Name the worksheet (and move it to the end):

Units sold-chart

The result may look like this.

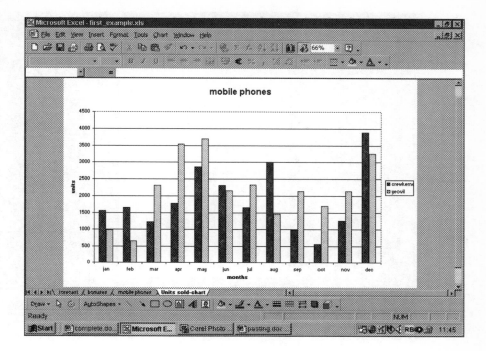

Click the **Copy** button, the chart should now be selected and you should see a moving dotted border around the chart to show that it has been selected.

Switch to the **Word** document.

Position the cursor underneath the data table and enter this text as a title:

Chart showing units sold

Position the cursor below this, pull down the **Edit** menu and select **Paste Special**, select **Picture** from the list and then **OK**.

> There are choices of format, **Picture** pastes as an image, **Excel Chart Object** creates an object which can be double-clicked and edited within Excel — the choice depends upon the end result desired (see also the section on **Linking**).

To size and centre the chart, **right-click** it and select **Format Picture** followed by **Size**.

Size it to fit on the page and then select the **Layout** tab.

Choose **In line with text** (**Wrapping style**), click **OK** and then use the **Center** button on the toolbar to centre the chart on the page.

Put a border around the chart and the previewed file in **Word** should now resemble this.

Save and close the files.

Linking Word and Excel files

If you link the worksheet data or chart you have pasted into Word then any changes to the original **Excel** file will automatically be reflected in the **Word** file.

To achieve this, you must use **Paste Special** and select the **Paste link** button.

Ⓐ *Activity*

Open a new **Word** document.

Save it, giving it the name **linking**, and then minimise the **Word** screen.

Open the Excel file **first_example** and select the worksheet named **forecast**.

Create a **column chart**, on a new sheet, from the data in the worksheet **forecast** using the data in cells **A2** to **G5**.

Add the **Chart title** (and suitable axis labels):

Sales & Profit Forecast

Format the chart as you wish.

Name the worksheet as **forecast-chart** and move it to the end.

Highlight all the data in the worksheet (**forecast**) and click on the **Copy** button.

Switch to the **Word** document.

Add a heading (format to choice):

A table showing sales for 2000

Position the cursor where you want the worksheet data to appear, pull down the **Edit** menu and select **Paste Special**.

There is a choice of pasting techniques, for example, you can paste it as a Microsoft Excel Worksheet Object, then it will be pasted as an object, which can be sized and moved around the screen (as with any object or picture).

This time make sure the following choices are made (especially **Paste link**); the data is pasted into **Word** as a table.

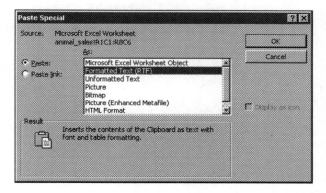

Format and centre the table.

Switch to the **Excel** worksheet and change the figure for the cell **B8** to:

150

Adjust column width as necessary, switch back to the **Word** document and you should see the change has automatically been made.

Switch to **Excel** and select the worksheet **forecast-chart**.

Click the **Copy** button, the chart should now be selected and you should see a moving dotted border around the chart to show that it has been selected.

Switch to the **Word** document.

Position the cursor underneath the data table and enter this text as a title, choosing a suitable format:

Chart showing sales

Position the cursor below this, pull down the **Edit** menu and select **Paste Special**, select **Paste link** and **Picture**.

To format the chart, **right-click** it and select **Format Object** followed by **Size**, within the **Scale** section enter **Height** and **Width** as **40%**.

Click the **Layout** tab, choose **In line with text** (**Wrapping style**), click **OK** and then use the **Center** button on the toolbar to centre the chart on the page.

Switch back to the **Excel** file and select the worksheet **forecast**.

Alter the figure for cell **D10** to read:

200

Select the chart (**forecast-chart**), double-click the X-axis and you will see the **Format Axis** dialog box, select the **Patterns** tab and then alter the **Tick mark labels** (tick **Low**) so that the columns do not obscure the X-axis labels.

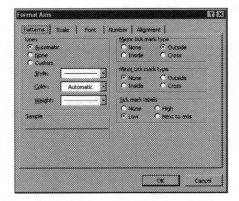

Switch back to the **Word** document and you should now see that both the worksheet and the chart have changed as a result of changing the figure.

The previewed file in **Word** should now resemble this.

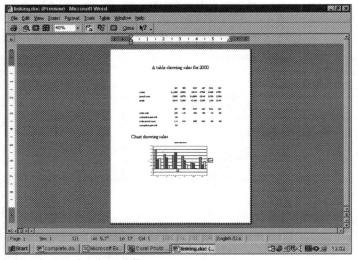

Save and close the Word and Excel files.

(E) **Exercise**

❑ Open a new **Word** document.

❑ Save the Word file, giving it the name **exercise_linking**.

❑ Open the Excel file **first_example** and select the worksheet **bonuses**.

❑ Create a column chart, on a new sheet, from the data in the worksheet **bonuses** using the data in cells **A2** to **D5**.

❑ Add suitable titles and format the chart as you wish.

❑ Name the worksheet as **bonuses-chart** (and move it to the end).

❑ Highlight all the data in the worksheet (**bonuses**) and click on the **Copy** button.

❑ Switch to the **Word** document and position the cursor where you want the worksheet data to appear.

❑ Pull down the **Edit** menu, select **Paste Special** and click **Paste Link**, pasting into Word.

❑ Centre the table and add a title (format to choice):

Table of bonuses

❑ Select the worksheet **bonuses-chart**.

❑ Click the **Copy** button.

❑ Switch to the **Word** document.

❑ Position the cursor underneath the data table and enter this text as a title:

Chart showing units sold

❑ Position the cursor below this, pull down the **Edit** menu and select **Paste Special**, select **Paste link** and **Picture**, click **OK**.

❑ Size and centre the chart.

❑ Switch to the **Excel** worksheet (**bonuses**) and change the figure for the cell **B3** to:

200

❑ Switch back to the **Word** document and you should now see that both the worksheet and the chart have changed.

The previewed file in **Word** should resemble this.

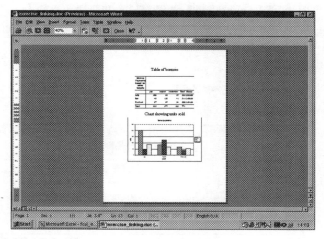

❑ Save and close all the files.

Linking worksheets

It is sometimes necessary to link the data in different worksheets, often because a formula within one worksheet refers to data in another.

(E) **Exercise**

❑ Begin a new Excel file, save it as **first_exercise** and enter the data.

	A	B	C	D	E
1	Denise's driving school				
2					
3		jan	feb	mar	Total
4	income				
5					
6	weekly cost per car				
7	wages				
8	total outgoings				
9					
10	income less total expenses				
11					
12		jan	feb	mar	
13	journeys	500	600	700	
14	average income per journey	20			
15	average cost per journey	10			
16	number of drivers	10	15	10	
17	weekly pay per driver	200	250	300	

❑ Enter formulas to calculate the

  • income (*journeys* multiplied by *average income per journey*)

  • weekly cost per car (*journeys* multiplied by *average cost per journey*)

  • wages (*number of drivers* multiplied by *weekly pay per driver*)

  • total outgoings (*weekly cost per car* added to *wages*)

  • income less total expenses (*income* less *total outgoings*)

  • the Total column

You **must** use absolute addressing for part of the formulas in rows **4** and **6**.

(T) A quick method of entering absolute references is to select the cell, select the cell references in the formula bar and press the **F4** key.

❑ Format the worksheet as you wish.

❑ Name the worksheet **costs 2000**.

The result should look like this.

	A	B	C	D	E
1	Denise's driving school				
2					
3		jan	feb	mar	Total
4	income	10000	12000	14000	36000
5					
6	weekly cost per car	5000	6000	7000	18000
7	wages	2000	3750	3000	8750
8	total outgoings	7000	9750	10000	26750
9					
10	income less total expenses	£ 3,000	£ 2,250	£ 4,000	£ 9,250

The formulas should be:

	A	B	C	D	E
1		Denise's driving school			
2					
3		jan	feb	mar	Total
4	income	=B13*$B$14	=C13*$B$14	=D13*$B$14	=SUM(B4:D4)
5					
6	weekly cost per car	=$B$15*B13	=$B$15*C13	=$B$15*D13	=SUM(B6:D6)
7	wages	=B16*B17	=C16*C17	=D16*D17	=SUM(B7:D7)
8	total outgoings	=SUM(B6:B7)	=SUM(C6:C7)	=SUM(D6:D7)	=SUM(B8:D8)
9					
10	income less total expenses	=B4-B8	=C4-C8	=D4-D8	=SUM(B10:D10)

❑ Save the file.

 Activity

You are going to use the original data to project into a new year by increasing the figures by a percentage.

Highlight the data in cells **A1** to **E10**, use the **Copy** button to copy it to *Sheet2* and call the new worksheet **costs 2001**.

The new worksheet will have zero values for the figures, highlight cells **B4** to **E7** and remove the contents (**Edit**, **Clear**, **Contents**).

Click in cell **B4** and begin to enter a formula by typing an = sign.

Select the original worksheet **costs 2000** and click in cell **B4**.

Add the following (before finishing the formula):

*110%

The formula should now read:

='costs 2000'!B4*110%

Enter this formula and copy it across the columns for the other months.

Carry out a similar exercise for the weekly cost per car (increase by 120%) and the wages (increase by 140%).

	A	B	C	D	E
1		Denise's driving school			
2					
3		jan	feb	mar	Total
4	income	11000	13200	15400	39600
5					
6	weekly cost per car	6000	7200	8400	21600
7	wages	2800	5250	4200	12250
8	total outgoings	8800	12450	12600	33850
9					
10	income less total expenses	£ 2,200	£ 750	£ 2,800	£ 5,750

The formulas should read as below (as you can see the formulas make reference to the other worksheet).

A	B	C	D
	Denise's driving school		
	jan	feb	mar
income	='costs 2000'!B4*110%	='costs 2000'!C4*110%	='costs 2000'!D4*110%
weekly cost per car	='costs 2000'!B6*120%	='costs 2000'!C6*120%	='costs 2000'!D6*120%
wages	='costs 2000'!B7*140%	='costs 2000'!C7*140%	='costs 2000'!D7*140%
total outgoings	=SUM(B6:B7)	=SUM(C6:C7)	=SUM(D6:D7)

Save and close the file.

Linking workbooks (files)

This follows the same principles as linking worksheets within a file. It can be useful, for example to consolidations.

Ⓐ **Activity**

To understand how this works, you are going to consolidate the data from **Denise's Driving School** into a new workbook.

Open the workbook **first_exercise**.

Open a new **Excel** file and save it as **exercise_consolidation**.

Rename *Sheet1* of this file **consolidation 2000-2001**.

Enter the following text (wrapping the text where appropriate), formatting the worksheet as you wish.

A	B	C	D	E	F	G
	Denise's driving school					
	income 2000	total outgoings 2000	profit 2000	income 2001	total outgoings 2001	profit 2001
jan						
feb						
mar						
total						

Click in cell **B3** and begin to enter a formula by typing an = sign.

Switch to the file **first_exercise** (**costs 2000** worksheet) and select the cell **B4**.

Click the **enter** button in the formula bar and you should automatically return to the **exercise_consolidation** workbook and see that the amount has been entered into the cell.

The formula shows that the cell contents in cell **B3** have been referenced to the originating workbook/worksheet.

='[first_exercise.xls]costs 2000'!$B$4

Enter the other figures for the *income* and *total outgoings* for 2000 and 2001 (be very careful to make sure you are referencing to the correct cell in the correct worksheet in the originating file).

Enter formulas to calculate the *profit* and *totals* and your worksheet should now look like this.

	A	B	C	D	E	F	G
1				Denise's driving school			
2		income 2000	total outgoings 2000	profit 2000	income 2001	total outgoings 2001	profit 2001
3	jan	10000	7000	3000	11000	8800	2200
4	feb	12000	9750	2250	13200	12450	750
5	mar	14000	10000	4000	15400	12600	2800
6	total	36000	26750	9250	39600	33850	5750

Save the file.

Any changes to the figures in the original file **first_exercise** will be automatically reflected in the consolidation.

You can try this **but** please **do not** save the changes you make.

Close all the open files.

Conditional formatting

In this section you will learn how to:

❑   Format cells according to their contents meeting certain criteria.

Excel contains a technique that enables you to format a cell depending upon a condition being met e.g. all cells below a certain value could be in italic or red or a different font size.

 Activity
Open the **exercise_consolidation** workbook. You may be asked if you want to update the workbook, click **Yes**.

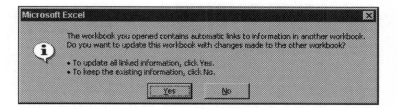

You are going to apply conditional formatting to the figures for the year 2001 so that they display in *red* if they are less than the corresponding figures for the year 2000.

Highlight the cells **E3** to **G5** and pull down the **Format** menu, select **Conditional Formatting**.

Enter the following, using the buttons within the dialog box to facilitate this.

The cell reference (**B3**) will initially be shown as an absolute reference, however you need this to be relative so that a comparison can be made between the corresponding figures for each year (so remove the **$** signs).

If you wanted your range to compare with the contents of a single cell then you would leave the reference as absolute.

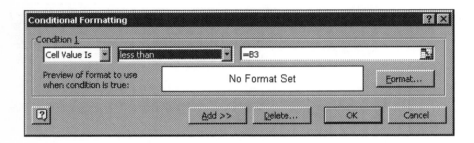

Click the **Format** button and select the format you want to impose on the cell (in this case alter the **Color** to **red**).

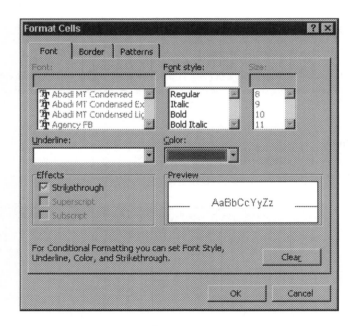

When you have finished, your worksheet should show certain figures in red (cells **G3** to **G5**) as they are less than the comparative figures for the previous year.

	A	B	C	D	E	F	G
1			Denise's driving school				
2		income	total outgoings	profit	income	total outgoings	profit
		2000	2000	2000	2001	2001	2001
3	jan	10000	7000	3000	11000	8800	2200
4	feb	12000	9750	2250	13200	12450	750
5	mar	14000	10000	4000	15400	12600	2800
6	total	36000	26750	9250	39600	33850	5750

To **Add** a condition to the previous condition, click the **Add > >** button within the **Conditional Formatting** dialog box.

Exercise

❑ Using the same cell range (**E3** to **G5**), add another condition to format all the cells that are *greater* than the corresponding figures in the previous year in ***bold blue italic***.

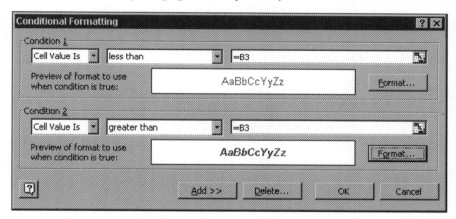

The result should now look similar to this.

	A	B	C	D	E	F	G
1			Denise's driving school				
2		income	total outgoings	profit	income	total outgoings	profit
		2000	2000	2000	2001	2001	2001
3	jan	10000	7000	3000	*11000*	*8800*	2200
4	feb	12000	9750	2250	*13200*	*12450*	750
5	mar	14000	10000	4000	*15400*	*12600*	2800
6	total	36000	26750	9250	39600	33850	5750

❑ Save and close the file.

Templates and protection

In this unit you will learn:

❑ What a template is

❑ How to create and save a template

❑ How to call up a template

❑ How to protect cells within a worksheet

❑ How to protect a complete worksheet

❑ How to hide formula

Templates

Templates can be used when you want worksheets or workbooks (files) to have common formatting, styles, macros etc.

Some of the features that can be included in a template are:

❑ Formatting commands

❑ Page Setup settings

❑ Repeated text

❑ Data, graphics, formulas, charts

Ⓐ **Activity**

Start a new file.

Highlight the whole worksheet by clicking the mouse in the top left corner of the worksheet where the rows and columns meet.

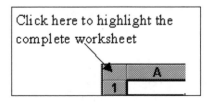

Change the font to **Times New Roman**.

Change the font size to **12** point.

Save the file as a **Template** (**File**, **Save As**, **Save as type**), calling it **font**, and close it.

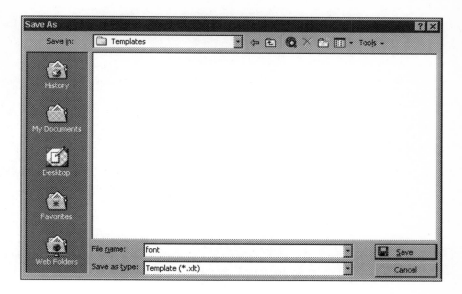

To use the template pull down the **File** menu and select **New**. The template should be shown.

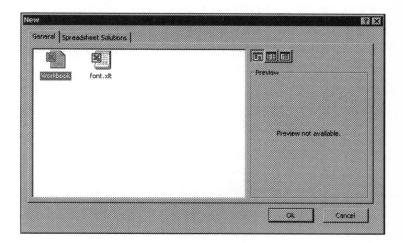

Select it and see how the default font type and size have been changed.

Close the file.

(E) Exercise

- ❑ Create a new file.
- ❑ Add the following features:
- ❑ Headers and footers (with your choice of contents).
- ❑ Column width (all columns) of 12

❏ Row height (all rows) of 15.

❏ Change the default font to **Arial 12** point.

❏ Save it as a template file called **Setup&format**.

❏ Close all the open files and then use the **File**, **New** to open a new file using this template.

❏ Close the file.

Protecting your work

If more than one person has access to a workbook or worksheet then it may be necessary to protect part or all of the worksheet/workbook so that it cannot be edited or altered.

Protecting cells

It is important to understand that the default is for cells to be **locked** as soon as you apply **protection** to the worksheet. Therefore if you wish certain cells or worksheets to remain accessible you must deliberately **unlock** them **before** applying **protection**.

 Activity

Open the workbook **first_exercise** and select the worksheet **costs 2000**.

Highlight cells **B14** and **B15**.

Pull down the **Format** menu, select **Cells**, and then the **Protection** tab. Clear the **Locked** check box so there is no tick in it.

These are the only cells in the worksheet that will be able to be changed or edited after you have protected the worksheet.

Pull down the **Tools** menu, then **Protection** and **Protect Sheet**.

You should see a dialog box, click **OK**.

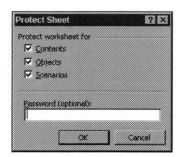

Save the file and then try to change any of the cells. You will find that the only cells that can be edited are **B14** and **B15**.

Hiding formulas

You can hide formulas so that the viewer cannot see them.

To hide formulas, the worksheet needs to be unprotected.

Activity

Pull down the **Tools** menu, then **Protection** and **Unprotect Sheet**.

Highlight all the cells with formulas in them (**B4** to **E10**), pull down the **Format** menu, select **Cells**, and then the **Protection** tab. Check the **Hidden** box so that it is ticked.

Now protect the sheet again by pulling down the **Tools** menu, then **Protection** and **Protect Sheet**.

The formulas should not be visible, so the viewer cannot see how the results were calculated.

Finally, pull down the **Tools** menu, then **Protection** and **Unprotect Sheet**. Close it *without* saving the changes.

Naming cells

In this unit you will learn:

❑   How to name cells

❑   How to use names in a formula

Cell names

As well as locating cells by their address, it is possible to give names to individual cells or groups of cells.

 Activity

Open the file **first_example** and view the worksheet **mobile phones**.

> As Excel does not accept names within formulas by default, pull down the **Tools** menu; select **Options**, and then **Calculation**.
>
> In **Workbook options**, click **Accept labels in formulas** so that it is ticked.

Highlight the cells **B4** to **B15**.

Pull down the **Insert** menu, followed by **Name** and **Define**.

You should see the dialog box shown (on the next page).

You can accept the name or change it.

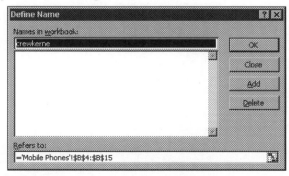

In this case, accept the settings.

Do the same for the next column, so you end up with names for all the data in the cells **C4** to **C15**.

Enter a title in cell **G3**:

total units sold

In cell **G4** begin a formula with the = sign.

Pull down the **Insert** menu, followed by **Name** and **Paste**. You will see a list of names you have created.

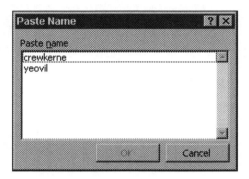

Select the first and click the **OK** button, type an addition sign (+) and pull down the **Insert** menu, followed by **Name** and **Paste** in the second name.

The formula should read:

=crewkerne+yeovil

Enter it and copy it down the column.

The result should look like this.

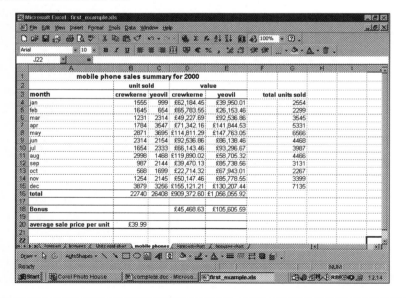

You could replace other cell references with appropriate names, for example in cell **B16**, you could enter the following formula:

=SUM (cɪewkerne)

Save and close the file.

Macros

In this unit you will learn:

❑   The purpose of macros

❑   How to record and run a macro

❑   How to assign a macro to a toolbar button

❑   How to delete a macro

What is a macro?

❑   A macro is a series of keystrokes and/or commands that is saved and can then be run at any time.

❑   This saves time and errors, as you merely need to call up and run the macro as opposed to entering what can be a complex series of keystrokes and commands.

❑   Macros can be assigned to a combination of keyboard characters or to a toolbar button, or they can be run using the **Tools** pull-down menu.

Recording and running a macro

 Activity

To record a macro you can use the **Macro Recorder**.

Start a new file and save it, giving it the name **second_example**.

Pull down the **Tools** menu, select **Macro**, then **Record New Macro**.

The dialog box will be displayed. Add the Macro name and shortcut key as shown below.

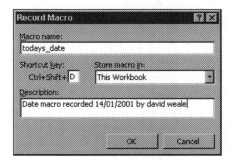

Note that when you enter the D in the **Shortcut key** box, the combination *may* change from just the **Ctrl** key to **Ctrl + Shift**. This is to avoid any conflict with existing key combinations. In Excel, many combinations of keyboard keys are already assigned, for example, the use of the **Ctrl** and **H** keys is assigned to the **Replace** command as a shortcut.

Click **OK** and begin to record the macro.

If the **Stop Recording** toolbar is not shown, pull down the **Tools** menu, followed by **Customize** and **Toolbars**. Tick **Stop Recording** and the toolbar will appear.

The default is for macro cell references to be absolute and the results of running a macro will appear in the cell that was the active cell when the macro was run. This allows the creation of formulas in macros that will relate to specific cells regardless of the position of the cursor when the macro is run. If you want a macro to select cells regardless of the position of the active cell when you run the macro then the cells can be made **relative**.

To make the cell references **relative**, click the **Relative Address** button on the **Stop Recording** toolbar so that it is pressed in (clicking it again when you want to return to using **absolute** cell references).

In this activity, you want the cell references to be **relative** so click the **Relative** button.

In the cell **A1**, enter the following text:

The date today is

In cell **A2** enter the **NOW** function (either pull down the **Insert** menu, then **Function** and find the function within **Date & Time** *or* use the **Paste Function** toolbar button).

Finally, stop the macro by clicking the **Stop** button on the toolbar or pulling down the **Tools** menu, selecting **Macro** and then **Stop Recording**.

You should now see the results of the macro on the screen.

	A	B
1	the date today is	
2	19/01/01 09:22	
3		

 Activity

To test this macro, open the file **first_example**, view the worksheet **mobile phones** and click the mouse in cell **A21**.

Pull down the **Tools** menu, select **Macro** and then **Macros**.

You should see a dialog box listing the macros.

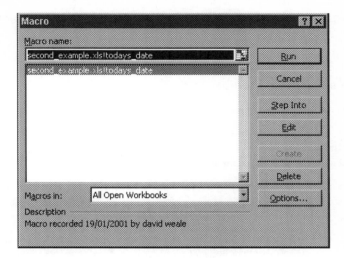

Select the macro you want to use and click the **Run** button.

The macro will be run and the results will appear in the worksheet.

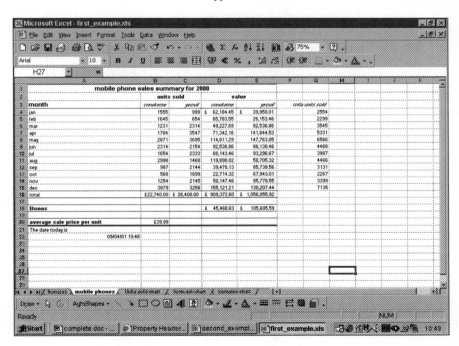

> If you are asked if you want to save the macro, in this case the answer is **Yes**. Alternatively, the **Recording Toolbar** will appear on the screen.

You need to be careful to either make sure the workbook in which you stored the macro is open or that you have selected that workbook in the **Macros in:** section of the **Macro** dialog box (see the illustration on the previous page) as macros are normally stored in the originating workbook.

Save and close all the open files

Assigning a macro to a toolbar button

You can assign a macro to a button on any visible toolbar.

 Activity

Open the file **second_example**.

You may see a dialog box asking if you want to **Enable Macros**, the reason for this is that macros may contain viruses and this is a way of avoiding destructive (or unknown) macros. In this case, you created the macro and can therefore enable it safely.

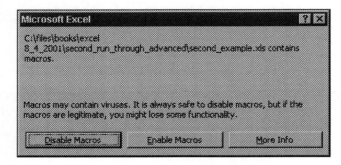

Pull down the **Tools** menu and select **Customize**, followed by **Commands**.

In the **Categories** list find **Macros** and drag the **Custom Button** onto any of the visible toolbars.

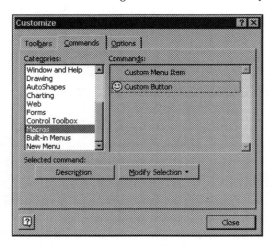

Right-click the macro button.

Select **Assign Macro**, and choose the macro (**todays_date**) you want to assign to the button from the list.

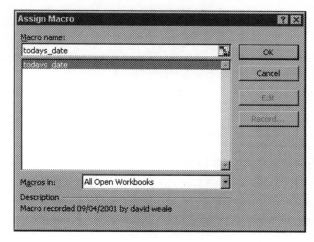

Finally, close the **Customize** dialog box, saving the file **second_example**.

Changing the toolbar button

If you have more than one macro assigned to the toolbar then each macro needs to be assigned to a different button image.

 Activity

Pull down the **Tools** menu and select **Customize**, followed by **Commands** (this must be visible before you can change the button image).

Right-click the macro button you have assigned to the toolbar and select **Change** **Button Image** from the list.

There is a variety of buttons to choose from.

Select one of these and close the dialog box.

Creating a text (macro) button

This is similar to an image.

 Activity

Make sure the **Customize** dialog box is visible and drag the **Custom Menu Item** onto a visible toolbar.

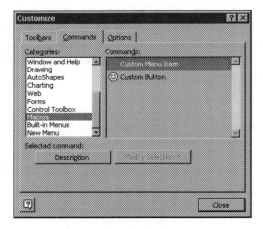

Right-click this button (on the toolbar) and change the text in the **Name** section to that shown below.

Close the **Customize** dialog box.

The toolbar should now show both the image button and the text button for your macro.

Save and close the file.

Deleting a macro

To delete a macro, you must first open the workbook in which the macro was saved, otherwise the macro name will not appear in the following dialog box.

Pull down the **Tools** menu, selecting **Macro** and then **Macros**.

Select the macro you want to delete and click the **Delete** button (in the **Macro** dialog box).

(E) *Exercise*

❑ Open the files **first_example** and **second_example**.

❑ Using the file **second_example**, create a new macro in *Sheet2*. This macro should be called **text_formatting_title** and should contain the following:

  • Relative cell referencing

  • Change the format applied to cell **A1** to **Times New Roman 16pt**

  • Change the format to wrap the text

❑ When you have stopped recording, switch to the file **first_example**, (**mobile phones** worksheet) click the mouse in cell **A1** and then run the macro you have created.

❑ The result may look like this.

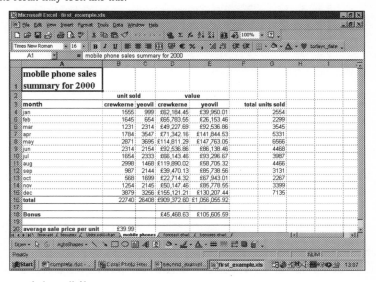

❑ Save and close all files.

(E) **Exercise**

❏ Open the workbook **second_example** and rename *Sheet3* as **page setup macro**.

❏ Create a macro called **page_setup**, assigned to keyboard characters **Ctrl** (+ **Shift** +) and **P** to carry out the following activities.

❏ Make the macro addressing **relative**.

❏ Use Page Setup to:

- Fit to one page and set to Landscape orientation.

- Centre the worksheet on the page.

- Add a header (your name) and footers (date and file name), change the fonts for these.

❏ Assign the macro to a new toolbar button.

❏ Begin a new workbook, entering some text and figures.

❏ Preview the worksheet.

❏ Run the macro you have just created (using the toolbar button).

❏ Preview the worksheet again and you should see that the macro has worked and the worksheet has taken on the characteristics contained in the macro.

❏ Save and close the file **second_example** and close the new file *without* saving the changes.

More functions

What you will learn about in this unit:

❏ Using nested IF statements

❏ Using the ROUND function

❏ Using financial function's (NPV, IRR)

❏ Using the Boolean operators AND, OR, NOT

❏ Using COUNT and COUNTIF

❏ Using MID, LEFT, RIGHT, LEN

Using nested IF statements

❏ You can nest **IF** statements to produce complex conditions. The structure is:

=IF(condition1, *IF(condition2, true, false)*, false)

❏ The inner IF statement (shown in italics) replaces the original **True** part of the function.

❏ If the original condition (*condition1*) is **true** then the second **IF** statement (*condition2*) is tested.

❏ If the original condition (*condition1*) is **false** then whatever is contained in the false section is carried out and the inner **IF** function is ignored.

Ⓐ Activity

You are given the following information concerning a business called Pamela's Products.

	jan	feb	mar	Total
Sales				
Purchases				
Total Wages				
Total Expenses				
Profit				
Bonus				
Units sold & purchased	500	600	700	
Sale price per/unit − sales	20			
Cost per/unit − purchases	10			
Number of salespersons	10	15	10	
Pay per salesperson	200	250	300	

Please create a new workbook, save it as **second_exercise**, with the layout shown above (right-align **row 1** and alter the width of **column A**).

Enter formulas to calculate the following, using **absolute** addresses where appropriate:

❑ The **Sales** figure is the number of *units sold* per month multiplied by the *sale price per/unit − sales*.

❑ The **Purchases** figure is the number of *units purchased* per month multiplied by the *cost price per/unit − purchases*.

❑ The **Total Wages** figure is the *number of salespersons* multiplied by the *pay per salesperson*.

❑ The **Total Expenses** is calculated by adding the *Purchases* and *Total Wages* figures.

❑ The **Profit** is the *Sales* minus the *Total Expenses*.

❑ Enter formulas to calculate the **Total** column.

❑ Insert two empty rows above **row 1** and in the first type the following title:

Pamela's Products

❑ Once you have entered the figures and the formulas, apart from the bonus, the worksheet should look similar to this, after you have formatted it as you wish.

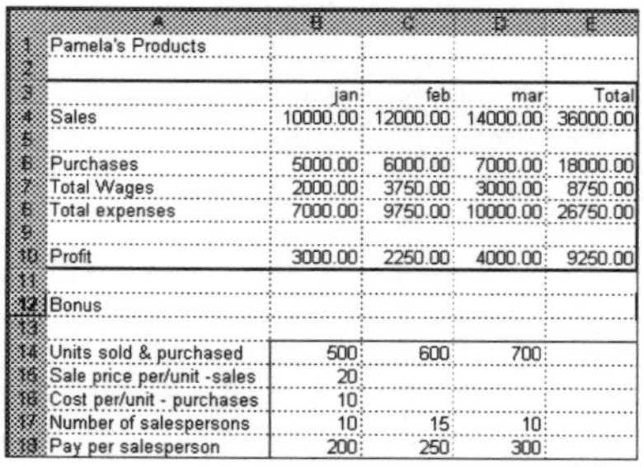

		A	B	C	D	E
1	Pamela's Products					
2						
3			jan	feb	mar	Total
4	Sales		10000.00	12000.00	14000.00	36000.00
5						
6	Purchases		5000.00	6000.00	7000.00	18000.00
7	Total Wages		2000.00	3750.00	3000.00	8750.00
8	Total expenses		7000.00	9750.00	10000.00	26750.00
9						
10	Profit		3000.00	2250.00	4000.00	9250.00
11						
12	Bonus					
13						
14	Units sold & purchased		500	600	700	
15	Sale price per/unit -sales		20			
16	Cost per/unit - purchases		10			
17	Number of salespersons		10	15	10	
18	Pay per salesperson		200	250	300	

> A bonus is paid on the following basis, if the total profit for the 3 months is greater than £10000 **and** the total wages bill is less than 50% of the total sales figure then a bonus of 5% of total sales is paid, otherwise no bonus is payable (use a nested conditional function).

Enter the following formula in cell **E12**:

=IF(E10>10000,IF(E7<50%*E4,E4*5%,0),0)

The bonus should be zero, why is this?

Think about this formula, what would happen if you altered the figure for the sale price per unit to £30. Would the bonus figure change?.

Change the sales price per unit to:

30

What is the bonus now?

Finally, apply the macro **text_formatting_title** (you need to have the file **second_example** open to do this) to cell **A1** and name the worksheet:

pamela's products

Format the worksheet and it may look similar to this.

Save and close all the files.

Ⓣ If you want to test for text, it is necessary to enclose the text in inverted commas (double speech marks), i.e. " ", **not** single marks, i.e. ' '.

Ⓣ Formulas are not case-sensitive (as you can see from the illustration following the next exercise).

E **Exercise**

❑ Open the workbook **second_exercise** and rename *Sheet2* as **Payroll**

❑ You are given the following data, enter it into the worksheet, format to choice.

	A	B	C	D	E	F	G
1	Pamela's Factory Payroll						
2							
3	Initial	Surname	Status	Hours Worked	Basic Pay	Overtime Pay	Total Pay
4	S	Smith	Skilled	44			
5	K	Yearn	Skilled	35			
6	L	Forest	Unskilled	15			
7	P	Justin	Skilled	53			
8	B	Erlish	Unskilled	32			
9	R	Borish	Unskilled	40			
10							
11	Pay is calculated using the following criteria						
12	**Status**		**Skilled**	**Unskilled**			
13	basic rate (first 40 hours)	£ 8.00	£ 6.00				
14	overtime rate	£ 12.00	£ 9.00				

❑ The *Basic Pay* and *Overtime Pay* are each calculated by testing if the person has worked over 40 hours, then testing the skill level for that employee (this is a fairly complex nested IF statement). You will also need to use **absolute addressing** in the formula (before copying it down).

❑ The *Total Pay* is worked out by adding the *Basic Pay* to the *Overtime Pay*.

❑ Sort the data into surname order.

❑ Total the data and present it in a professional manner.

The final worksheet could look like this.

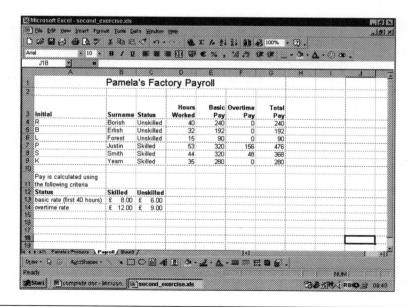

The formulas are shown below.

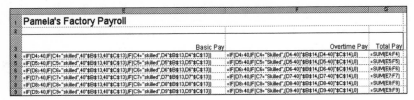

Pamela's Factory Payroll		
	Basic Pay	Overtime Pay	Total Pay
=IF(D4>40,IF(C4="skilled",40*$B$13,40*$C$13),IF(C4="skilled",D4*$B$13,D4*$C$13))	=IF(D4>40,IF(C4="Skilled",(D4-40)*$B$14,(D4-40)*$C$14),0)	=SUM(E4:F4)
=IF(D5>40,IF(C5="skilled",40*$B$13,40*$C$13),IF(C5="skilled",D5*$B$13,D5*$C$13))	=IF(D5>40,IF(C5="Skilled",(D5-40)*$B$14,(D5-40)*$C$14),0)	=SUM(E5:F5)
=IF(D6>40,IF(C6="skilled",40*$B$13,40*$C$13),IF(C6="skilled",D6*$B$13,D6*$C$13))	=IF(D6>40,IF(C6="Skilled",(D6-40)*$B$14,(D6-40)*$C$14),0)	=SUM(E6:F6)
=IF(D7>40,IF(C7="skilled",40*$B$13,40*$C$13),IF(C7="skilled",D7*$B$13,D7*$C$13))	=IF(D7>40,IF(C7="Skilled",(D7-40)*$B$14,(D7-40)*$C$14),0)	=SUM(E7:F7)
=IF(D8>40,IF(C8="skilled",40*$B$13,40*$C$13),IF(C8="skilled",D8*$B$13,D8*$C$13))	=IF(D8>40,IF(C8="Skilled",(D8-40)*$B$14,(D8-40)*$C$14),0)	=SUM(E8:F8)
=IF(D9>40,IF(C9="skilled",40*$B$13,40*$C$13),IF(C9="skilled",D9*$B$13,D9*$C$13))	=IF(D9>40,IF(C9="Skilled",(D9-40)*$B$14,(D9-40)*$C$14),0)	=SUM(E9:F9)

- ❏ Save and close the file.

Using the ROUND function

- ❏ This is a very useful function as it rounds decimal figures to the desired number of decimal places (there are variations on the theme such as ROUNDUP and ROUNDDOWN).

Ⓐ **Activity**

Open the file **first_example** and look at the worksheet **bonuses**.

Enter the following into the worksheet cells, beginning in cell **A8**.

8	value	rounded value
9	2.335	
10	2.459	
11	2.513	
12	2.999	

- ❏ Click in cell **B9** and click the **Paste Function** button, selecting **Math & Trig** from the **Functions category** and **ROUND** from the list of **Function names**.
- ❏ Enter the following data into the dialog box.

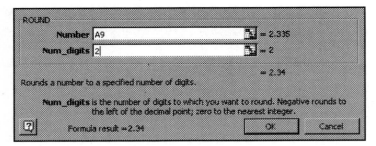

- ❏ Copy this formula down to cell **B12**.
- ❏ You can now see clearly how the rounding works (I have formatted the figures in **column B** to two decimal places).

8	value	rounded value
9	2.335	2.34
10	2.459	2.46
11	2.513	2.51
12	2.999	3.00

❑ Enter the following labels into the given cells.

C8	roundup
D8	rounddown

(E) *Exercise*

❑ In cells **C9** and **D9** use the **ROUNDUP** and **ROUNDDOWN** functions to round the figures in **column A** (to 2 d.p.).

❑ Copy these formulas down to the other cells.

❑ The result should look like this.

8	value	rounded value	roundup	rounddown
9	2.335	2.34	2.34	2.33
10	2.459	2.46	2.46	2.45
11	2.513	2.51	2.52	2.51
12	2.999	3.00	3.00	2.99

❑ Consider how the different functions work.

❑ Save the file.

Applying the ROUND function to other functions

Using the same worksheet, you are going to round the **bonus** figures calculation.

Firstly, edit the formula in **F3** to read as follows:

=IF(E3>250,E3*0.999,E3*0.499)

Copy this down to the other two cells in the column and format all three cells to 3 decimal places .

	A	B	C	D	E	F
1	Bonus Payments based on sales targets					
2		july	august	september	Total	Bonus
3	Sally	200	85	67	352	£ 351.648
4	Ben	45	125	41	211	£ 105.289
5	Rachael	87	67	54	208	£ 103.792
6	Total	332	277	162	771	

Now to round the calculations using the **ROUND** function.

It is probably easiest to edit the formula (to add the **ROUND** function) manually, edit the cell **F3** to read.

=IF(E3>250,**ROUND (E3*0.999,2),ROUND(E3*0.499,2))**

Copy this down the column and then reformat the cells to 2 decimal places.

The result should look like this.

	A	B	C	D	E	F
1	Bonus Payments based on sales targets					
2		july	august	september	Total	Bonus
3	Sally	200	85	67	352	£ 351.65
4	Ben	45	125	41	211	£ 105.29
5	Rachael	87	67	54	208	£ 103.79
6	Total	332	277	162	771	

Save and close the file.

Using financial functions

Within Excel, several functions enable you to evaluate projects and carry out financial analysis.

This section deals with using Excel to calculate the **NPV** (Net Present Value) and **IRR** (Internal Rate of Return).

These techniques are often used to compare projects so that a choice can be made.

NPV

This technique calculates the return from a project using *discounted* values (it is assumed that money could be invested instead of being used to finance the project, so the return on that money has to be taken into account).

 Activity

Start a new file, save it as **finances** and enter the following data into a worksheet (renaming this as **npv**), format appropriately.

	A	B	C	D	E
1			project one		
			cash	cash	net	present
2	year		inflow	outflow	cashflow	value
3		0		6000		
4		1	3000	1500		
5		2	4000	1300		
6		3	5500	2500		
7		4	4500	2000		
8	discounted value					
9	net present value					
10	discount rate					

Enter a formula in cell **D3** to calculate the **net cashflow** (the *cash inflow* **minus** the *cash outflow*) and copy this down.

In cell **E3**, enter a formula to make this cell equal to the cell **D3**.

In cell **B10**, enter the figure:

15%

In cell **E8**, use the **Paste Function** button to enter a **NPV** function (this is in the **Financial** category), entering the following data.

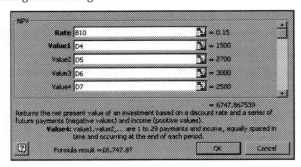

This function uses the cell containing the *discount rate* and then the cells containing the individual *net cashflow* for each year, this calculates the discounted value for each year using the rate of interest in cell **B10**.

In cell **E9** enter a formula to add the figures in that column, it should read:

=E8+E3

This calculates the **net** present value for the cashflow, if it is positive then the return from the project exceeds what could have been earned by investing the money in a bank paying 15% interest.

The result should look like this:

	A	B	C	D	E
1			project one		
2	year	cash inflow	cash outflow	net cashflow	net present value
3	0		6000	-6000	-6000
4	1	3000	1500	1500	
5	2	4000	1300	2700	
6	3	5500	2500	3000	
7	4	4500	2000	2500	
8	discounted value				£6,747.87
9	net present value				£747.87
10	discount rate	15%			

The formulas are shown below for reference.

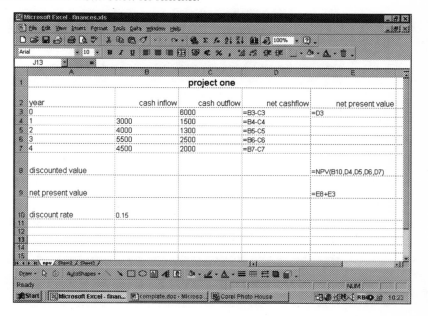

(E) **Exercise**

❑ Rename *Sheet2* as npv_new_project.

❑ Enter the following data and calculate the net present value of the project.

❑ Compare this with the results from **project one**, the project with the higher NPV is the more profitable.

	year	cash inflow	cash outflow	net cashflow	net present value
	0		14000		
	1	9000	4000		
	2	10000	6000		
	3	7000	2000		
	4	8000	4000		
Discounted Value					
Net Present Value					
Discount Rate		12%			

project two

The resulting figures should look like this.

	year	cash inflow	cash outflow	net cashflow	net present value
	0		14000	-14000	-14000
	1	9000	4000	5000	
	2	10000	6000	4000	
	3	7000	2000	5000	
	4	8000	4000	4000	
Discounted Value					£13,754
Net Present Value					-£ 246
Discount Rate		12%			

project two

The formulas should look like this.

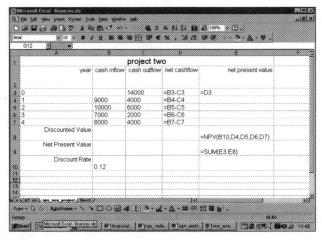

	year	cash inflow	cash outflow	net cashflow	net present value
0			14000	=B3-C3	=D3
1		9000	4000	=B4-C4	
2		10000	6000	=B5-C5	
3		7000	2000	=B6-C6	
4		8000	4000	=B7-C7	
Discounted Value					=NPV(B10,D4,D5,D6,D7)
Net Present Value					=SUM(E3:E8)
Discount Rate		0.12			

project two

❑ Save the file.

IRR

This function calculates the rate of return from a project, i.e. if the IRR of a project is higher than the cost of borrowing money then it is a worthwhile project (and has a positive NPV).

This function is another way of quantifying the return from a project and deciding if the project is worthwhile.

(A) Activity

Return to the worksheet **npv** and enter in cell **A11** the word IRR.

In cell **E11**, enter the **IRR** function using the following data.

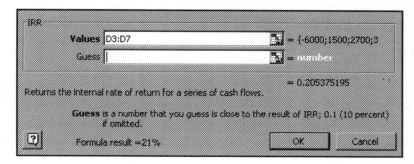

It is not normally necessary to enter a **Guess** figure.

The result is shown below.

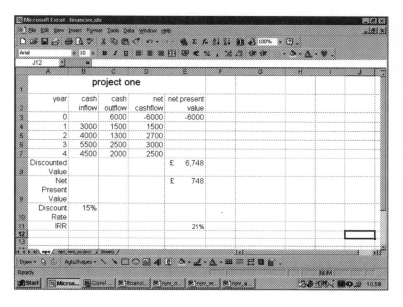

(E) Exercise

❑ Calculate the IRR for the other project in the worksheet **npv_new_project**.

The result is shown below.

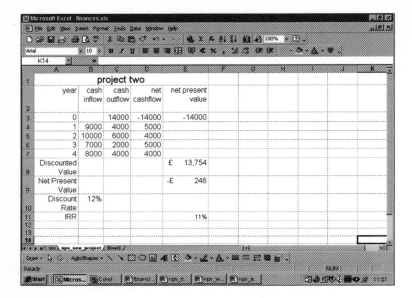

❑ Save and close the file.

Using the operators AND, OR, NOT

AND

This tests whether arguments (up to 30) are true.

The result will return **False** unless **all** the arguments are true.

=AND(argument1, argument2, argument3, . . .)

Examples

=AND(*true, true*) returns TRUE e.g. =AND(8+2=10, 6-3=3) equals TRUE

=AND(*true, false*) returns FALSE e.g. =AND(3+3=6, 2+1=4) returns FALSE

You can test whether cells contain specific data, for example, if you want to test whether the cell **A1** contains a number between 50 and 60, the function could read:

=AND(A1>=50, A1<=60)

The result should return TRUE if the cell A1 contains a figure between 50 and 60, otherwise it will return FALSE.

 Activity

Open the workbook **second_example** (enable macros if you are asked) and rename *Sheet1* as **macro-example**.

Move to *Sheet2* and rename it as **AND-example**.

In cell **A1**, enter the following:

=AND(8+2=10, 6-3=3)

If this has been entered correctly, the cell should read TRUE as both arguments are true.

In cell **A2**, enter:

=AND(3+2=6, 2+2=4)

If this has been entered correctly, the cell should read FALSE as one of the arguments is not correct.

Now you want to test whether any number you enter in cell **A3** is between 50 and 60.

In cell **A3**, enter the following:

=AND(B3>=50, B3<=60)

Now in cell **B3** enter the values (one at a time), 49, 50, 51, 60, 61 to see the result in cell **A3**.

Save the file.

Combining AND and IF functions

You can combine the **AND** function and the **IF** function.

Activity

Suppose you want a figure to appear in a cell only if the value of the figure is in a certain range, and for a message to appear if this is not so.

For example, you may want to test whether **B4** contains a number between 30 and 45, and to display a message if it does not.

In cell **A4**, enter the following formula:

=IF(AND(B4>30, B4<45), "correct", "wrong")

This tests firstly the AND function, testing whether the value in **B4** is greater than 30 **and** less than 45, then **if** this is true "*correct*" will appear in cell **A4**, otherwise the message "*wrong*" will appear.

Test this by entering figures into **B4** to see what message appears in **A4**.

OR function

This tests whether any of the arguments are **True**.

=OR(argument1, argument2, argument3, ...)

The result will only return **False** if **all** the arguments are false.

Examples

=OR(*true, true*) returns TRUE *e.g.* =OR(8+2=10, 6-3=3) returns TRUE

=OR(*true, false*) returns TRUE *e.g.* =OR(3+3=6, 2+1=4) returns TRUE (as one of the arguments is true)

(A) Activity

Insert a new worksheet (**Insert**, **Worksheet**) naming it **OR-example**.

In cell **A1**, enter the following:

=OR(8+2=10, 6-3=3)

If this has been entered correctly, the cell should read TRUE as both of the arguments are true.

In cell **A2**, enter:

=OR(3+2=6, 2+2=4)

If this has been entered correctly, the cell should read TRUE as one of the arguments is true.

In cell **A3**, enter the following:

=OR(8+2=11, 6-3=2)

If this has been entered correctly, the cell should read FALSE as neither of the arguments is correct.

Save the file.

NOT function

The NOT function can be used when you want to make sure a value is not equal to another value.

If the argument is **False**, NOT returns TRUE; if the argument is **True**, the NOT function returns FALSE.

Examples

=NOT(2+3=5) equals FALSE
=NOT(2+1=5) equals TRUE

(A) Activity

Insert a new worksheet (**Insert**, **Worksheet**) naming it **NOT-exercise** and moving to the end.

In cell **A1**, enter the following:

=NOT(2+3=5)

In cell **A2**, enter the following:

=NOT(2+1=5)

Are the results correct?

Save and close the file.

(E) Exercise

❏ Open the workbook **second_exercise**.

❏ View the worksheet **Payroll**.

□ Enter the following text in cell **H3**:

Skilled & Worked Overtime

□ Enter a formula (using the IF and AND functions) in cell **H4** to test whether the worker is skilled *and* the number of hours worked is over 40, then print the message (**yes**) if this is true, and a message (**no**) if it is not true.

□ Copy this down (using **AutoFill**) to the other cells in the column.

The worksheet answer is shown below, followed by the formula.

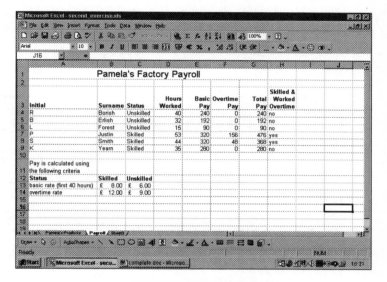

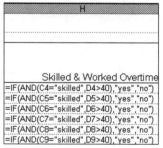

H
Skilled & Worked Overtime
=IF(AND(C4="skilled",D4>40),"yes","no")
=IF(AND(C5="skilled",D5>40),"yes","no")
=IF(AND(C6="skilled",D6>40),"yes","no")
=IF(AND(C7="skilled",D7>40),"yes","no")
=IF(AND(C8="skilled",D8>40),"yes","no")
=IF(AND(C9="skilled",D9>40),"yes","no")

□ Save and close the file.

COUNT and COUNTIF

□ These functions count how many cells contain data.

 Activity

□ Open the workbook **second_exercise** and view the worksheet **Payroll**.

❏ Enter text into the following cells, and format the cells to wrap text.

E11	number of workers
E12	number of skilled workers
E13	number of unskilled workers

❏ In cell **F11**, enter the following function (this is contained in the **Statistical** category if you are using the **Paste Function** button).

=COUNT(D4:D9)

This counts the number of cells in the range **D4** to **D9** that contain a number. It can only be used with cells containing numeric data.

In cell **F12**, use the **Paste Function** button to enter the COUNTIF function and use the button to enter the data shown below.

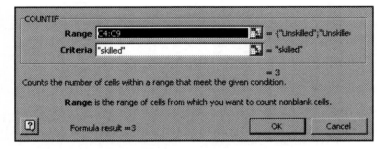

This function counts the number of cells that contain the word skilled.

The results should look like this.

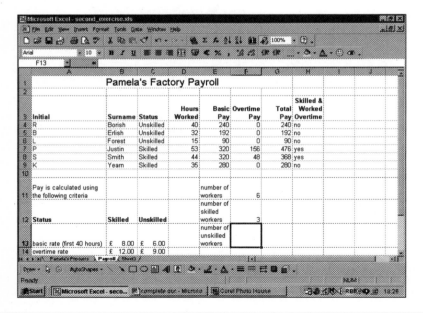

Exercise

❏ Enter a function in cell **F13** to count the number of cells that contain the word **unskilled**.

❏ Alter the text in cell **C6** to read **skilled**.

❏ The values in cells **F12** and **F13** should change, as should the pay calculations and totals in the row.

The results should look similar to this.

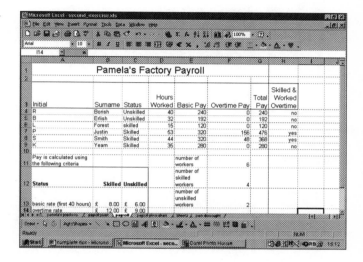

The formulas are shown below.

	E	F
11	number of workers	=COUNT(D4:D9)
12	number of skilled workers	=COUNTIF(C4:C9,"skilled")
13	number of unskilled workers	=COUNTIF(C4:C9,"unskilled")

❏ Save and close the file.

MID, LEFT, RIGHT and LEN functions

These functions make it easier to extract information and can be applied to any data (numeric, alphabetic or alphanumeric).

Activity

Open a new file, save it as **third_example** and rename *Sheet1* as **strings**.

In this worksheet, enter the following data.

	A	B	C	D	E	F
1	name	LEFT	RIGHT	MID	LEN	surname
2	b.smith					
3	d.giles					
4	h.abbot					
5	j.devott					
6	k.smith					
7	l.atkins					
8	r.hunter					

LEFT

This function selects a number of characters from the left of the cell contents.

(A) **Activity**

In cell **B2**, enter the following (using the **Paste Function** button – you will find the **LEFT** function in the **Text** category).

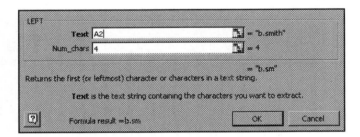

The formula should read as follows (it selects the first 4 characters of the entry, from the left, this includes characters such as full stops):

=LEFT (A2,4)

Copy the function down the column; the result should look like this.

	A	B
1	name	LEFT
2	b.smith	b.sm
3	d.giles	d.gi
4	h.abbot	h.ab
5	j.devott	j.de
6	k.smith	k.sm
7	l.atkins	l.at
8	r.hunter	r.hu

RIGHT

This function selects a number of characters from the right of the cell contents.

(A) **Activity**

In cell **C2,** enter the following (using the **Paste Function** button).

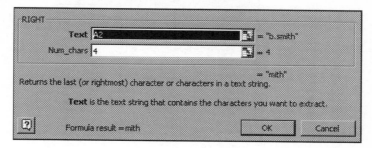

The function will look like this (it selects the last 4 characters from the string).

=RIGHT (A2,4)

Copy the function down the column; the result should look like this.

	A	B	C
1	name	LEFT	RIGHT
2	b.smith	b.sm	mith
3	d.giles	d.gi	iles
4	h.abbot	h.ab	bbot
5	j.devott	j.de	vott
6	k.smith	k.sm	mith
7	l.atkins	l.at	kins
8	r.hunter	r.hu	nter

MID

This function selects a number of characters from the cell contents starting at a specified character numbered from the left.

(A) **Activity**

In cell **D2,** enter the MID function (using the **Paste Function** button).

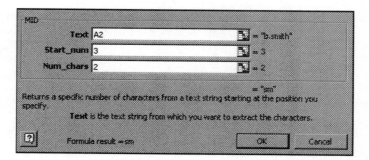

The function will look like this (the function selects two characters starting at the third character in from the left).

=MID (A2,3,2)

53

Copy the function down the column; the result should look like this.

	A	B	C	D
1	name	LEFT	RIGHT	MID
2	b.smith	b.sm	mith	sm
3	d.giles	d.gi	iles	gi
4	h.abbot	h.ab	bbot	ab
5	j.devott	j.de	vott	de
6	k.smith	k.sm	mith	sm
7	l.atkins	l.at	kins	at
8	r.hunter	r.hu	nter	hu

LEN

This function counts the number of characters making up the cell contents.

(A) Activity

In cell **E2**, enter the following (using the **Paste Function** button).

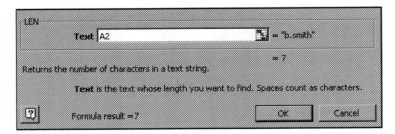

The function will look like this.

=LEN (A2)

Copy the function down the column; the result should look like this.

	A	B	C	D	E
1	name	LEFT	RIGHT	MID	LEN
2	b.smith	b.sm	mith	sm	7
3	d.giles	d.gi	iles	gi	7
4	h.abbot	h.ab	bbot	ab	7
5	j.devott	j.de	vott	de	8
6	k.smith	k.sm	mith	sm	7
7	l.atkins	l.at	kins	at	8
8	r.hunter	r.hu	nter	hu	8

Save the file.

Combining the functions

You may want to extract specific data from a cell, here is an example of how two functions can be combined to achieve a certain result.

In this case, we want to extract the surname so that the data can be sorted in surname order.

Activity

Enter the following function in cell **F2** and copy it down the column.

=RIGHT (A2,LEN (A2)-2)

This should have the effect of entering the surname into the cells (it works out the length of the string, deducts 2 from that value and then selects that number of characters from the right of the string, thus missing out the first two (left) characters in the string).

Sort the data into surname order and your result should look like this.

	A	B	C	D	E	F
1	name	LEFT	RIGHT	MID	LEN	surname
2	h.abbot	h.ab	bbot	ab	7	abbot
3	l.atkins	l.at	kins	at	8	atkins
4	j.devott	j.de	vott	de	8	devott
5	d.giles	d.gi	iles	gi	7	giles
6	r.hunter	r.hu	nter	hu	8	hunter
7	b.smith	b.sm	mith	sm	7	smith
8	k.smith	k.sm	mith	sm	7	smith

Save and close the file.

Pivot tables

In this unit you will learn about:

❑ How to create a pivot table

❑ Formatting a pivot table

❑ Creating a chart from a pivot table

Pivot tables can be used to arrange and summarise large and complex tables of data.

A pivot table is interactive and you rearrange the rows and columns to view the data in different combinations.

 Activity

Open the file **third_example**, enter the data into *Sheet2* and name the worksheet **pet food**.

Pauline's Pet Emporium			
Order Book			
supplier	date of order	product	order amount
pet ancillaries	17-Jun-00	sand	11
pets & ponds	18-Jun-00	fish food	36
pets & ponds	06-Sep-00	fish food	30
pets & ponds	11-Nov-00	fish food	41
pets & ponds	11-Nov-00	fish food	33
pet ancillaries	15-Nov-00	sand	6
pet ancillaries	16-Nov-00	sand	33
domestic cleaning supplies	19-Nov-00	fullers earth	56
pets & ponds	30-Nov-00	fish food	65

Creating a pivot table

Highlight the cells **A3** to **D12,** pull down the **Data** menu, select **Pivot Table and PivotChart Report**.

You will see the following dialog box.

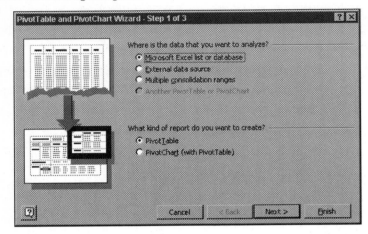

Accept the default choices (shown above) and click the **Next** button to move on.

Assuming you have highlighted the correct range of cells, this should read as in the illustration below (if it does not click the button on the right and click and drag the mouse to select the correct range of cells).

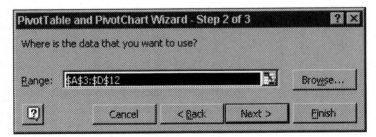

The next choice is to decide where you want to place the new pivot table , it is usually best to put it in a new worksheet (the default).

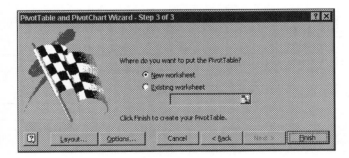

Finally, click the **Finish** button and a worksheet will appear with the framework of the pivot table.

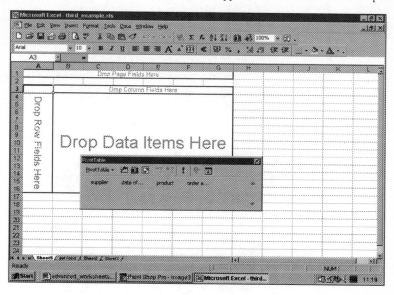

You drag the field names (**supplier**, **date of**, **product** and **order amount**) from the **Pivot Table** toolbar onto the pivot table itself.

Initially, drag the **product** field to **Drop Row Fields Here** and drag the **order amount** field to **Drop Data Items Here**.

The result should look like this.

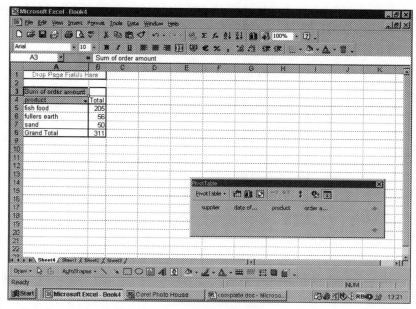

Now drag the **supplier** field to the **Drop Page Fields Here** (cell **A1**).

The display will change, pull down the list of suppliers (**row 1**) by clicking the arrow to the right of (**All**).

Select the first supplier (**domestic cleaning supplies**) and click **OK**

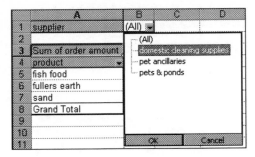

The pivot table should now display the data for only that supplier.

A	B
1 supplier	domestic cleaning supplies ▼
2	
3 Sum of order amount	
4 product ▼	Total
5 fullers earth	56
6 Grand Total	56

Rearranging the pivot table

By dragging the field names from the toolbar onto the pivot table or from the pivot table back to the toolbar, you can rearrange the contents of the table.

For example, drag the **supplier** field off the table and then drag the **date of order** field onto the table in its place and pull down the list of order dates.

Your pivot table should now look like this.

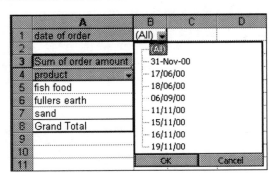

You can now look at the data by date and see the total order for each product for any of the order dates.

Name this worksheet **pet food pivot** and position to the right of the original **pet food** worksheet.

Drag fields on and off the pivot table to experiment with the various ways in which you can rearrange the data.

The pivot table toolbar

The toolbar should appear whenever you are looking at a worksheet with a pivot table in it. If the toolbar fails to appear, pull down the **View** menu, select **Toolbars** followed by **PivotTable**.

The full toolbar will only appear when you select the pivot table by clicking within it.

Formatting the pivot table

(A) *Activity*

Click within the pivot table, click the **Format Report** button (in the **PivotTable** toolbar), and select **Report 3**.

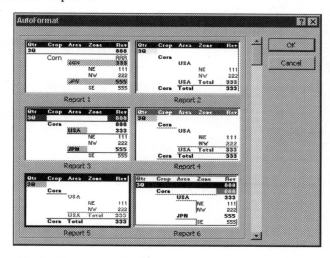

Your pivot table should now resemble this.

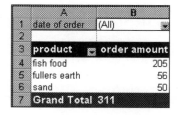

Save and close the file.

Exercise

❑ Open the file **second_exercise** and view the worksheet **payroll**.

❑ Highlight the data in cells **A3** to **G9** and create a pivot table using the following fields.

Drop Page Fields Here	Status
Drop Row Fields Here	Surname
Drop Data Items Here	Total Pay

❑ Use the **Report Format** button to format the report, the result may look like this.

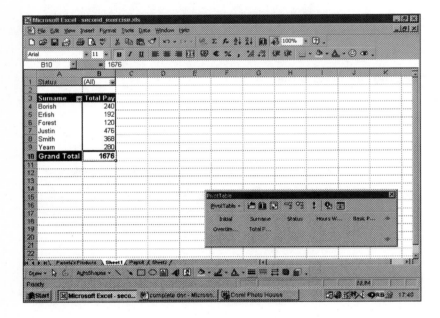

❑ Name the worksheet **payroll pivot**.

Charting pivot tables

Charts can be produced automatically from pivot tables with the advantage that the chart contains pull-down lists for the data fields so that you can look at the chart data in the same way as you can look at the original pivot table.

 Activity

Click within the pivot table you have just created and click the **Chart** button on the **Pivot Table** toolbar.

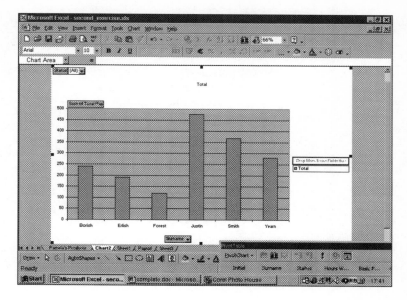

A chart will appear, pull down the lists for each data item (click the arrow to the right of each) and see how the chart automatically changes to reflect your choices (remove the tick from any items in the list you do not want to appear in the chart).

When you have finished experimenting, name the worksheet containing the chart as **payroll pivot chart** and move it to the right of the **payroll** worksheet.

Save and close the file.

The Lookup functions

In this unit you will learn about:

❑ The purpose of Lookup functions

❑ The different types of Lookup (LOOKUP, VLOOKUP and HLOOKUP)

❑ How to use the Lookup function

These functions enable you to extract data from worksheet lists . When you know the value in one column/row, you can find the corresponding value in another column/row.

For example, if you have a list of descriptions and prices, you can find the price of an item by entering the description.

LOOKUP

This finds a value in one row or column (sorted into *ascending* order) and then returns the value in the same position in a different row or column.

Activity

Open a new file and save it as **fourth_example**.

Add the following table.

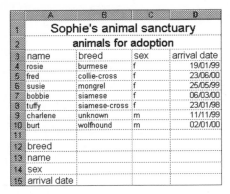

	A	B	C	D
1	Sophie's animal sanctuary			
2	animals for adoption			
3	name	breed	sex	arrival date
4	rosie	burmese	f	19/01/99
5	fred	collie-cross	f	23/06/00
6	susie	mongrel	f	25/05/99
7	bobbie	siamese	f	06/03/00
8	tuffy	siamese-cross	f	23/01/98
9	charlene	unknown	m	11/11/99
10	burt	wolfhound	m	02/01/00
11				
12	breed			
13	name			
14	sex			
15	arrival date			

Format the worksheet using **AutoFormat**.

Position the cursor in cell **B13**.

Click the **Paste Function** button on the toolbar.

Select the **Lookup & Reference** category and then **Lookup** from the list on the right.

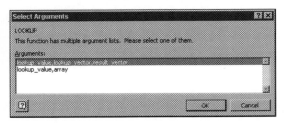

Usually the **LOOKUP** function will use the **vector** argument (an explanation of the differences is available in the Excel on-screen **Help**).

A vector is a row or column.

Use the buttons to enter the following data.

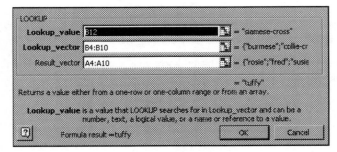

You should see a **#N/A** message in cell **B13** at this point as no data has been entered into the breed lookup value, in cell **B12**.

> Cell **B12** will eventually contain the breed you want to look up, cells **B4** to **B10** contain the list of breeds and cells **A4** to **A10** contain the names of the animals corresponding to the breed.
>
> The idea is that you enter a breed in cell **B12** and the name of the animal corresponding to that breed will appear in cell **B13**.

(T) For the **LOOKUP** function to work properly the **Lookup vector** (in this case **B4** to **B10**) **must** be sorted into ascending order.

Position the cursor in cell **B12** and enter:

siamese-cross

Cell **B13** should now contain the **name** of the animal (column A) corresponding to that breed.

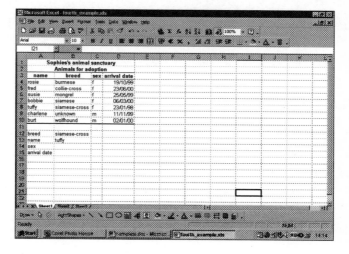

(E) **Exercise**

❑ Enter into cell **B14** a **LOOKUP** function to look up the **sex** corresponding to the **breed** entered in cell **B12**.

❑ Enter into cell **B15** a **LOOKUP** function to look up the **arrival date** corresponding to the breed entered in cell **B12**, you may need to format **B15** to display a date format (**Format, Cells, Number, Date**).

	A	B	C	D
1	Sophie's animal sanctuary			
2	Animals for adoption			
3	name	breed	sex	arrival date
4	rosie	burmese	f	19-Oct-99
5	fred	collie-cross	f	23-Jun-00
6	susie	mongrel	f	25-May-99
7	bobbie	siamese	f	6-Mar-00
8	tuffy	siamese-cross	f	23-Jan-98
9	charlene	unknown	m	11-Nov-99
10	burt	wolfhound	m	2-Jan-00
11				
12	breed	siamese-cross		
13	name	tuffy		
14	sex	f		
15	arrival date	23-Jan-98		

The formulas look like this.

	A	B
1	Sophie's animal sanctuary	
2	Animals for adoption	
3	name	breed
4	rosie	burmese
5	fred	collie-cross
6	susie	mongrel
7	bobbie	siamese
8	tuffy	siamese-cross
9	charlene	unknown
10	burt	wolfhound
11		
12	breed	siamese-cross
13	name	=LOOKUP(B12,B4:B10,A4:A10)
14	sex	=LOOKUP(B12,B4:B10,C4:C10)
15	arrival date	=LOOKUP(B12,B4:B10,D4:D10)

❑ Name the worksheet as **animals** and save the file.

VLOOKUP

This looks in the first column of an array or table for a value and finds the corresponding value in the specified column.

 Activity

Using the worksheet **animals**, copy and paste the data in cells **A1** to **D10** into *Sheet2* and rename *Sheet2* as **animals-vlookup**.

Enter the following data into the specified cells.

A12	name
A13	breed

Sort the data on column **A** into ascending order (otherwise the function will not work correctly as the table has to be sorted in ascending order of the initial column).

Click in cell **B13** and select the **Paste Function** button on the toolbar.

Select the **Lookup & Reference** category and then **VLOOKUP** from the list on the right.

Enter the following data (using the buttons at the right of each row).

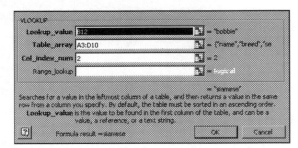

This means that you will eventually enter the name of an animal in cell **B12** and the function will look up the corresponding breed (**column 2**) from the array **A3** to **D10**.

Enter in cell **B12**:

bobbie

The breed for this animal should appear in cell **B13**.

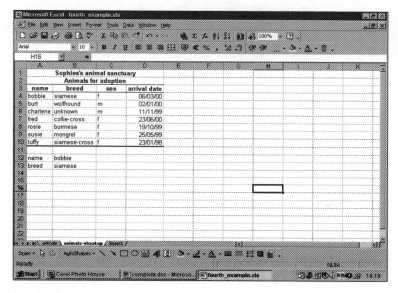

Try this with other names.

(E) **Exercise**

❑ In cell **A14** enter the word:

Sex

❑ Enter a **VLOOKUP** function in cell **B14** to display the sex for the name you enter in cell **B12**.

❑ Format the worksheet.

The result should look like this.

The formulas are shown below.

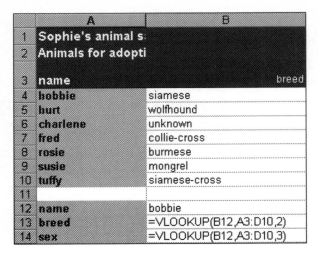

	A	B
1	Sophie's animal s:	
2	Animals for adopti	
3	name	breed
4	bobbie	siamese
5	burt	wolfhound
6	charlene	unknown
7	fred	collie-cross
8	rosie	burmese
9	susie	mongrel
10	tuffy	siamese-cross
11		
12	name	bobbie
13	breed	=VLOOKUP(B12,A3:D10,2)
14	sex	=VLOOKUP(B12,A3:D10,3)

❑ Save the file.

HLOOKUP

This looks for a value in the top row of an array (table) and returns the corresponding value from the specified row.

 Activity

You are going to transpose the data using a new technique before creating the function.

Transposing data

Highlight the data in cells **A3** to **D10** of the worksheet **animals-vlookup**, click the **Copy** button and move to *Sheet3*.

Position the cursor in cell **A1** and pull down the **Edit** menu, selecting **Paste Special**.

You will see the **Paste Special** dialog box, select (tick) **Transpose**.

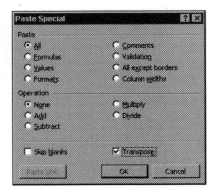

Enter the following data in the given cells (using the **Format**, **Column**, **AutoFit Selection**) to AutoFit the data.

A6	name
A7	arrival date

Rename *Sheet3* as **animals-hlookup**.

The worksheet should now look like this.

	A	B	C	D	E	F	G	H
1	name	bobbie	burt	charlene	fred	rosie	susie	tuffy
2	breed	siamese	wolfhound	unknown	collie-cros	burmese	mongrel	siamese-cross
3	sex	f	m	m	f	f	f	f
4	arrival date	6-Mar-00	2-Jan-00	11-Nov-99	23-Jun-00	19-Oct-99	25-May-99	23-Jan-98
5								
6	name							
7	arrival date							

In cell **B7**, enter the following data (using the **HLOOKUP** function).

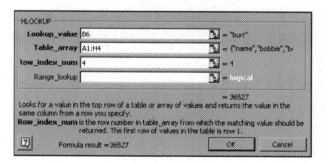

Format cell **B7** to **Date**.

In cell **B6**, enter the following name:

burt

The result should look like this.

	A	B	C	D	E	F	G	H
1	name	bobbie	burt	charlene	fred	rosie	susie	tuffy
2	breed	siamese	wolfhound	unknown	collie-cros	burmese	mongrel	siamese-cross
3	sex	f	m	m	f	f	f	f
4	arrival date	6-Mar-00	2-Jan-00	11-Nov-99	23-Jun-00	19-Oct-99	25-May-99	23-Jan-98
5								
6	name	burt						
7	arrival date	2-Jan-00						

Enter other names into cell **B6** to test the function.

Save and close the file.

Exercise

❑ Open the file **second_exercise** and look at the worksheet **payroll**.

❑ Enter data into cells as follows.

A16	Name
A17	Status
A18	Hours Worked
A19	Total Pay

❑ In the cells **B17** to **B19**, enter **LOOKUP** functions so that when a **surname** is entered into cell **B16** the data that relates to that person automatically appears.

❑ Test the functions by entering different names into **B16** (remembering that the data needs to be sorted by **column B** – the lookup vector).

The result should correspond to this.

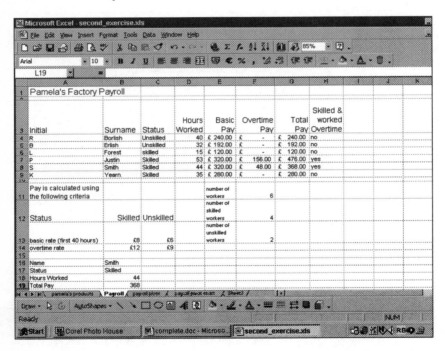

The formulas I have used are shown below (however if you have used a different **LOOKUP** function and it works this is fine).

16	Name	Smith
17	Status	=LOOKUP(B16,B4:B9,C4:C9)
18	Hours Worked	=LOOKUP(B16,B4:B9,D4:D9)
19	Total Pay	=LOOKUP(B16,B4:B9,G4:G9)

❑ Save and close the file.

Viewing and formatting worksheets

In this unit you will learn about:

❑ Freezing parts of the worksheet

❑ Splitting the worksheet

❑ Setting print areas

❑ Setting page breaks

❑ Repeating row and column labels

❑ Adding comments to worksheets

Freezing parts of the worksheet

If you have a large worksheet, extending beyond the boundaries of the screen, you may want to freeze parts of the screen.

 Activity

Open the file **second_exercise**, look at the worksheet **Pamela's Products**.

Freezing horizontally

Select **row 4**, pull down the **Window** menu and select **Freeze Panes**.

This freezes the screen horizontally, all the rows above **row 4** remain static, and when you scroll only the bottom part of the screen will move. Remove this by pulling down the **Window** menu and selecting **Unfreeze Panes**.

Freezing vertically

Select **column B**, pull down the **Window** menu and select **Freeze Panes**.

This freezes the screen vertically, all the rows to the left of **column B** remain static, and when you scroll only the right part of the screen moves.

Remove this by pulling down the **Window** menu and selecting **Unfreeze Panes**.

Freezing horizontally and vertically

Click the mouse in cell **B4**, pull down the **Window** menu and select **Freeze Panes**.

This freezes the screen horizontally, all the rows above **row 4** remain static and vertically, **column A** remains static while the other columns scroll.

With this technique, you need to click the mouse in the cell below and to the right of the position where you want the split to appear.

Remove this by pulling down the **Window** menu and selecting **Unfreeze Panes**.

How to split the worksheet

This is a different technique with a similar purpose. This enables you to split the screen so that you have two (or more) views on the same worksheet, **both** of which can be scrolled.

 Activity

Use the file **second_exercise** and the worksheet **pamela's products**.

Splitting horizontally

Select **row 4**, pull down the **Window** menu and select **Split**.

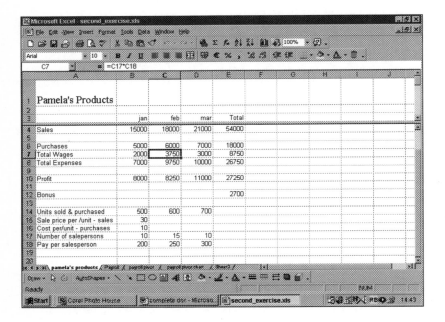

This splits the screen horizontally; each part of the screen can be scrolled independently.

Remove this by pulling down the **Window** menu and selecting **Remove Split**.

Splitting vertically

Select **column B**, pull down the **Window** menu and select **Split**.

This splits the screen vertically; each part of the screen can be scrolled independently.

Remove this by pulling down the **Window** menu and selecting **Remove Split**.

Splitting horizontally and vertically

Click the mouse in cell **B4**, pull down the **Window** menu and select **Split**.

This splits the screen horizontally and vertically; each part of the screen can be scrolled independently.

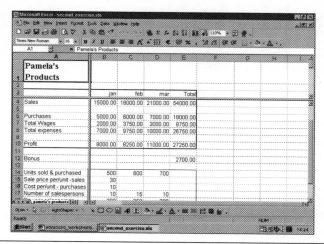

> With this technique, you need to click the mouse in the cell below and to the right of the position where you want the split to appear.

(T) You can drag the dividers within the split screen to new positions if you wish.

Remove this by pulling down the **Window** menu and selecting **Remove Split**.

Setting print areas

You can determine which area of the worksheet you want to print (perhaps because you do not want the reader to see part of the worksheet).

(A) *Activity*

Using the file **second_exercise** and the worksheet **pamela's products**, highlight the area **A1** to **E10**.

Pull down the **File** menu, select **Print Area** and **Set Print Area**.

Select the **Print Preview** button (only the selected area of the worksheet will be displayed or printed).

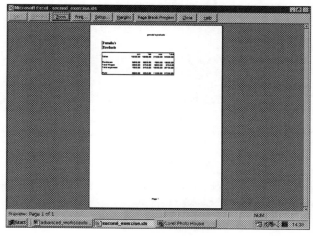

Remove the setting by pulling down the **File** menu, selecting **Print Area** followed by **Clear Print Area**.

If your worksheet is not printing out in its entirety, it may be that you have set the print area by mistake. Follow the procedure above to clear this if necessary.

Close the file *without* saving the changes.

Setting page breaks

Excel will automatically set page breaks for printing; unfortunately, these may not be where you want the page to break and the new page to begin.

Activity

Open the file **second_exercise** and the worksheet **payroll**.

Pull down the **View** menu and **Page Break Preview**; you should see a rather different view of your worksheet.

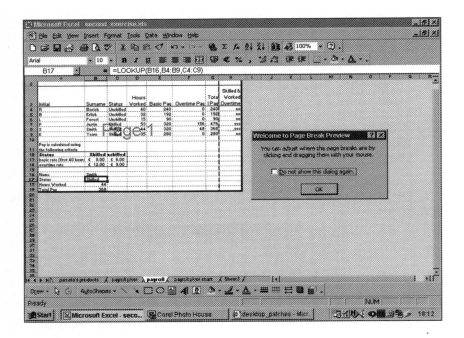

This shows the page breaks within the worksheet as dashed lines either vertically or horizontally.

Inserting page breaks

You can insert horizontal or vertical page breaks by selecting the row or column **after** the column or row where you want the break to appear.

Page breaks can be inserted in **Normal** or **Page Break Preview** views.

Activity

Select **column D** and pull down the **Insert** menu, selecting **Page Break**.

The page break will be positioned to the left of **column D**, thus splitting the worksheet into two pages.

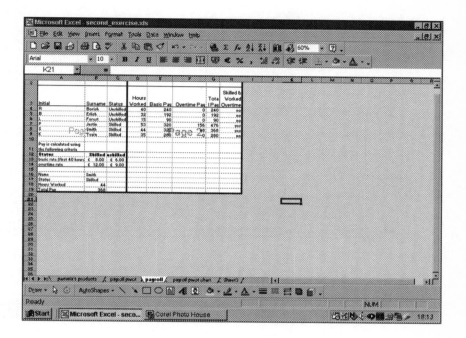

Removing page breaks

To remove a page break, select the column (to the right) or row (below) the page break, pull down the **Insert** menu and select **Remove Page Break**.

 Activity

Remove the page break you have just inserted.

Repeating row and column labels

If your worksheet prints over several sheets then you may want print either (or both) row and column labels on every page.

 Activity

Insert a page break above **row 7** so that your worksheet is split into two pages.

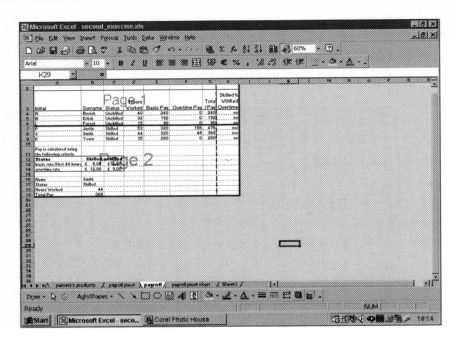

Pull down the **File** menu, select **Page Setup** followed by **Sheet**.

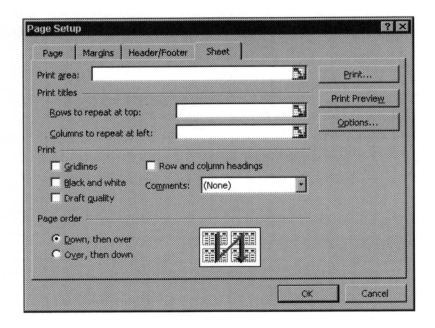

You want the headings in **row 3** to repeat on every page, so click the button at the end of the **Rows to repeat at top** box.

Select **row 3**, at which point the screen should look like this.

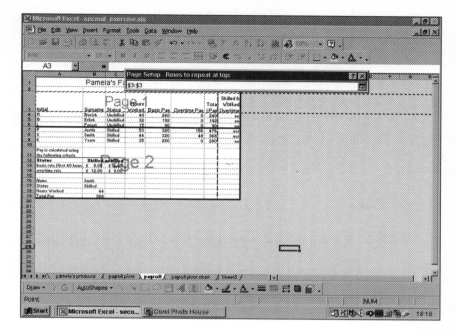

Click the button on the end to return to the dialog box and then **OK** to return to the worksheet.

 The repeated columns do **not** appear in this view but will display if you click the **Print Preview** button.

Save and close the file.

Adding comments to worksheets

It can be very useful to add comments to a worksheet, which are only visible when desired.

This is different from using text boxes, which are always visible; a comment is only visible when the mouse pointer hovers over the cell containing the comment.

 Activity

Open the file **second_example** (worksheet **page setup macro**).

Select cell **A1**, pull down the **Insert** menu and select **Comment**.

A comment box will appear, enter the following text:

this worksheet contains a macro to automate page setup

When you have finished, click elsewhere on the sheet, all that is visible is a small red triangle in the top right-hand corner of the cell, denoting a comment.

When the mouse pointer hovers over the cell, the comment becomes visible.

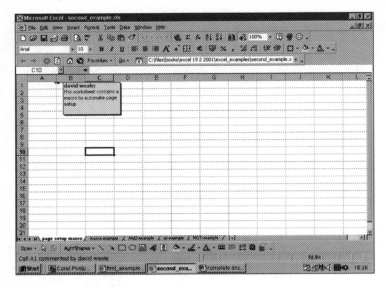

Right-clicking the cell displays a menu allowing you to carry out activities with the comment e.g. edit, delete or show the comment.

Save and close the file.

What-If analysis

In this unit you will learn about:

❑ The purpose of input tables

❑ Creating one-variable input tables

❑ Using the Fill Series technique

❑ Creating two-variable input tables

❑ Using Goal Seek

❑ Using Solver

❑ Creating and managing scenarios

Input tables

A data table shows how changing different values within the formulas will affect the result of those formulas.

Data tables are a quick and easy way of carrying out several calculations at once and of seeing the results of different input values on the same worksheet, thus what happens as a result of differing input values.

You can create a **one-variable** data table or a **two-variable** data table.

One-variable data tables

An example of how these can be used is to calculate the effect of a change in the interest rate on monthly loan repayments and/or the total amount repaid.

Data tables can be based on either **rows** or **columns**, i.e. the input values have to be listed down a column or across a row.

 Activity

Begin a new workbook, save it as **projections** and rename *Sheet1* as **one-variable input**.

Enter the data shown below, formatting the figures to the number of decimal places shown and the text as you wish.

	Loan Repayments Table			
Number of months for repayments	60			
Amount of loan	£ 1,200			
	Interest Rates	Monthly Repayments	Total Amount Repaid	
Repayment at	9.00%			
Other interest rates	5.00%			

Fill Series

Excel contains a useful technique to fill in data incrementally.

 Activity

Highlight cells **B6** to **B20**; pull down the **Edit** menu, select **Fill** followed by **Series**.

Enter the following data into the dialog box.

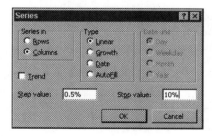

The data will fill the cells from **B6** (value **5%**) to **B16** (value **10%**) in steps or increments of **0.5%**.

You may need to format the cells to 2 decimal places.

Name the cells given below as follows (**Insert**, **Name**, **Define**):

B2	Months
B3	Loan
B5	Interest_rate

In cell **C5**, enter the following formula (a quick and accurate way of entering cell names into a formula is to click on the cell (name) rather than type it in).

=PMT (interest_rate/12, months, -loan)

This calculates the amount that needs to be paid every month on the loan at the specified rate of interest and is one of the financial functions (other such as NPV and IRR are explained in another section).

To complete the table, highlight the cells **B5** to **C16**, pull down the **Data** menu and select **Table.**

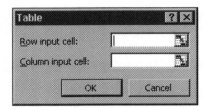

Use the button at the end of the dialog box to select cell **B5** (as the input variables are listed down the column, you use the **Column input cell.**

Note that the reference is **absolute.**

You should now see the input table completed, format the cells in column **C** to **currency** with **2 decimal places**.

	A	B	C	D
1	Loan Repayments Table			
2	Number of months for repayments	60		
3	Amount of loan	£ 1,200		
4		Interest Rates	Monthly Repayments	Total Amount Repaid
5	Repayment at	9.00%	£24.91	
6	Other interest rates	5.00%	£22.65	
7		5.50%	£22.92	
8		6.00%	£23.20	
9		6.50%	£23.48	
10		7.00%	£23.76	
11		7.50%	£24.05	
12		8.00%	£24.33	
13		8.50%	£24.62	
14		9.00%	£24.91	
15		9.50%	£25.20	
16		10.00%	£25.50	

To make use of the table, alter the input data, i.e. the *Number of months for repayments*, the *Amount of the loan* or the *Repayment at* (rate of interest).

To finish the table, enter a formula in cell **D5** to calculate the *Total Amount Repaid* (the *Monthly Repayments* multiplied by the *Number of months for repayments*) and copy this down the column.

(T) An advantage of using **named** cells is that it avoids the need for **absolute referencing**.

Format the figures in the same way as you formatted **column B** and the result should look like this.

	A	B	C	D
1	Loan Repayments Table			
2	Number of months for repayments		60	
3	Amount of loan	£	1,200	
4			Interest Rates	Monthly Repayments	Total Amount Repaid
5	Repayment at		9.00%	£24.91	£1,494.60
6	Other interest rates		5.00%	£22.65	£1,358.73
7			5.50%	£22.92	£1,375.28
8			6.00%	£23.20	£1,391.96
9			6.50%	£23.48	£1,408.76
10			7.00%	£23.76	£1,425.69
11			7.50%	£24.05	£1,442.73
12			8.00%	£24.33	£1,459.90
13			8.50%	£24.62	£1,477.19
14			9.00%	£24.91	£1,494.60
15			9.50%	£25.20	£1,512.13
16			10.00%	£25.50	£1,529.79

Save the file.

Two-variable tables

This differs from the one-variable table in that there are two variables (one variable goes down a column and the other variable across a row).

Thus a two-variable table creates a two-dimensional matrix.

(A) *Activity*

Rename *Sheet2* as **two-variable input** and enter the following data, using **Fill (Series)** to enter the figures.

	A	B	C	D	E	F
1	Bonus Scheme Payment Schedule					
2						
3	total monthly sales (less than)		Bonus rate (percentage of total sales)			
4			1%	2%	3%	4%	5%
5		1000					
6		1500					
7		2000					
8		2500					
9		3000					
10		3500					
11		4000					
12		4500					
13		5000					

Click the mouse pointer in cell **A4** and enter the formula

=G1*G2

> The cell references for the input values (**G1** and **G2**) can be any empty cells. They are simply used for reference in the table dialog box and have no effect on the results.
>
> However, the cell holding the formula **must** be cell **A4** as this is the cell positioned above the column data and to the left of the row data.

To create the table, highlight cells **A4** to **F13** and pull down the **Data** menu, select **Table**.

The **row input cell** will be **G1** and the **column input cell G2**.

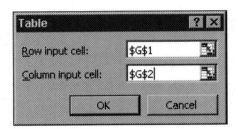

The table should now be complete.

Creating a two-variable input table is a quick method of carrying out repetitive calculations.

Bonus Scheme Payment Schedule

total monthly sales (less than)	Bonus rate (percentage of total sales)				
	1%	2%	3%	4%	5%
0					
1000	10	20	30	40	50
1500	15	30	45	60	75
2000	20	40	60	80	100
2500	25	50	75	100	125
3000	30	60	90	120	150
3500	35	70	105	140	175
4000	40	80	120	160	200
4500	45	90	135	180	225
5000	50	100	150	200	250

Save and close the file.

Goal Seek

This technique is useful when you know the answer you want to arrive at, but do not know the input value.

Using **Goal Seeking**, the input value is calculated from the result you want to achieve.

(A) **Activity**

Open the file **projections** and rename *Sheet3* as **goal seeking**.

Enter the following data into the worksheet, formatting as you wish.

	A	B
1	Calculation of required markup to achieve a specific profit figure	
2	cost per item	10
3	markup	25%
4	sale price per item	
5	expected number of items sold	2000
6	total profit	

In cell **B4**, enter a formula to calculate the *sale price per item* (the *cost per item* plus the calculated *markup* figure), e.g.

=B2+B2*B3

In cell **B6**, enter a formula to calculate the *total profit* (*sale price per item* multiplied by the *expected number of items sold*).

The worksheet should now contain these figures.

	A	B
1	Calculation of required markup to achieve a specific profit figure	
2	cost per item	£ 10.00
3	markup	25%
4	sale price per item	£ 12.50
5	expected number of items sold	2000
6	total profit	£ 25,000.00

You are now going to use **Goal Seek** to find out the mark-up (and therefore the sale price per item), to achieve a total profit of £30,000.

Pull down the **Tools** menu and select **Goal Seek**.

Use the buttons within the dialog box to select the cells shown in the illustration below.

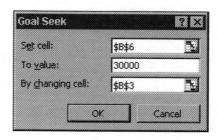

The mark-up figure should now change to that required to achieve the proposed profit figure.

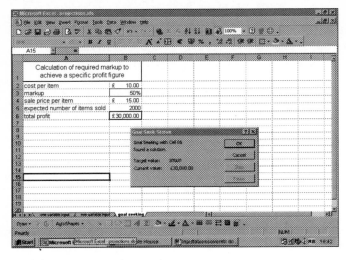

At this point, click **OK** to accept the new figures.

Save and close the file.

Solver

Solver is another problem-solving technique, allowing you to find the best combination of values to achieve the desired result.

It is also possible to set constraints on the chosen variables (e.g. maximum and minimum values).

Solver will analyse the problem and arrive at the best combination of figures to achieve the desired result. With this tool changes can be made to more than one variable.

 Activity

Open the file **projections** and create a copy of the worksheet **goal seeking**, naming it **solving**.

Ensure the figures are as shown below (by altering cells **B3** and **B5**, if necessary).

A	B
Calculation of required markup to achieve a specific profit figure	
cost per item	£ 10.00
markup	25%
sale price per item	£ 12.50
expected number of items sold	2000
total profit	£ 25,000.00

This time we want to achieve a total profit of £30,000 but with certain constraints imposed on the mark-up and expected number of items sold.

Pull down the **Tools** menu, selecting **Solver**.

Enter the following data into the dialog box, using the buttons as necessary. **Add** the constraints shown (by clicking the **Add** button) and tick the **Value of** circle.

Use the **Ctrl** key (together with the mouse) to select more than one cell in the **By Changing Cells** box.

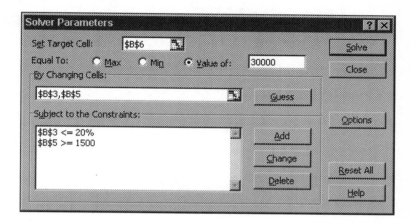

Finally, click the **Solve** button and the program will arrive at its solution to the problem.

At this point, a dialog box is displayed asking if you want to keep the new figures or revert to the original and whether you want to save the **Scenario** enabling you to use the cell contents with the **Scenario Manager**.

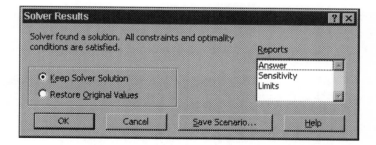

Elect to keep the Solver solution and save the **Scenario** calling it **profits**.

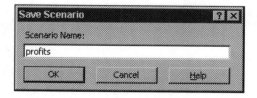

Solver can also produce reports (shown in the right side of the **Solver Results** dialog box) and if you select any of these, they will be printed on a new worksheet.

Select the **Answer** report, an example of the report produced is shown below.

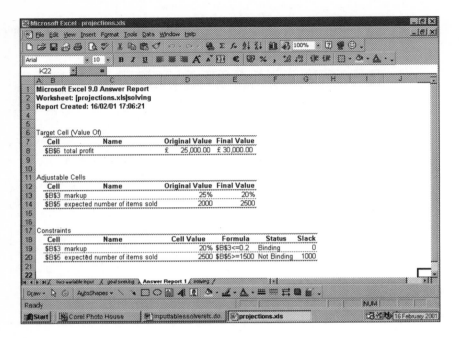

Rename this worksheet as **solver report**.

(E) *Exercise*

❑ Using the same worksheet (**solving**) create a new scenario using the following data.

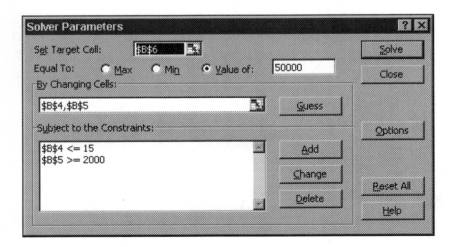

❑ Save the scenario as **profit second**.

The results should look similar to this.

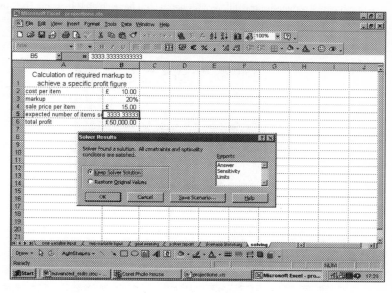

❑ Save and close the file.

Scenario Manager

This tool can be used with saved **Solver** solutions. You can save as many solutions as you want and then use the **Scenario Manager** to view them, print them or make changes to them.

(A) *Activity*

Open the file **projections** and view the worksheet **solving**.

Pull down the **Tools** menu and select **Scenarios**. The **Scenario Manager** dialog box will be displayed.

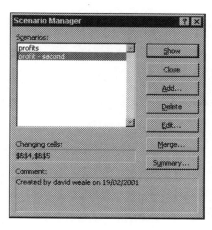

You can select any of the available scenarios, add, delete, edit, merge, or summarise scenarios.

Creating summaries from scenarios

You can easily summarise the different scenarios you have created by using the **Summary** button (in the **Scenario Manager** dialog box).

Select the **Scenario Summary** option.

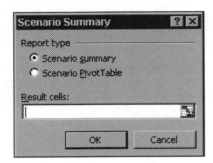

(T) There is no need to enter a figure for the **Result cells** when selecting the **Scenario Summary** option.

Click **OK** and the results are written to a new worksheet (shown below).

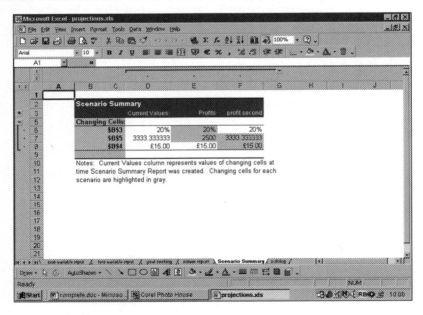

Save and close the file.

Auditing and validating data

In this unit you will learn about auditing and:

❑ Using the auditing tools

❑ How to check and validate data entry

Auditing

Excel comes with powerful tools to enable you to find errors in the design of the worksheet or in the use of formulas in your worksheets e.g. circular references. A circular reference is where the cell containing the answer is mistakenly included within the formula.

 Activity

Start a new file and save it as **auditing & validation**.

Pull down the **Tools** menu, select **Auditing** followed by **Show Auditing Toolbar**.

The various buttons are described below.

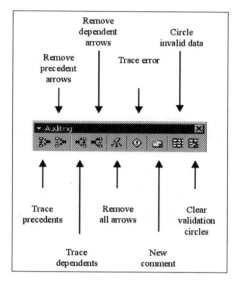

Enter the following data, formatting as you wish (but keeping the same cell references), and rename the worksheet as **auditing**.

	A	B	C	D
1	carols café			
2	total number of items sold			
3	total income			
4				
5	products	average unit price	sold per week	total income
6	meals	£ 5.15	500	
7	tea	£ 0.60	2600	
8	coffee	£ 0.90	1900	

Enter formulas to calculate:

❏ **total income** – (cells **D6** to **D8**) (*average unit price* multiplied by *sold per week*)

❏ **total number of items sold** – cell **B2** (sum of *sold per week*)

❏ **total income** – cell **B3** (sum of *total income* cells)

❏ The results should look like this.

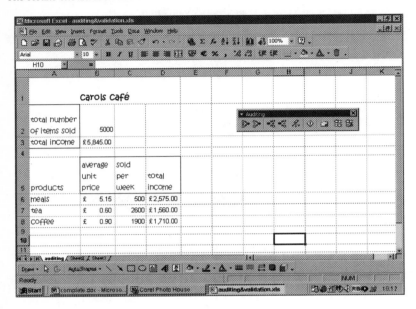

The formulas should be as shown below.

	A	B	C	D
1		Carols Café		
2	total number of items sold	=SUM(C6:C8)		
3	total income	=SUM(D6:D8)		
4				
5	products	average unit price	number sold per week	total income
6	meals	5.15	500	=B6*C6
7	tea	0.6	2600	=B7*C7
8	coffee	0.9	1900	=B8*C8

Tracing precedents

Tracing the precedents (those cells making up a formula) of a cell involves selecting the cell with the formula in it and then clicking the **Trace Precedents** button on the **Auditing** toolbar.

Ⓐ **Activity**

Select cell **B3** and click the **Trace Precedents** button. A blue tracer arrow should appear showing the cells making up the formula in **B3**.

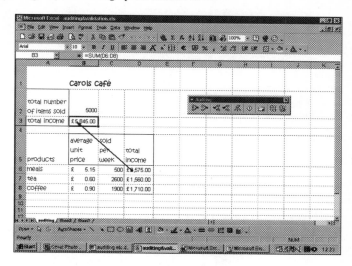

Remove the arrow (**Remove Precedent Arrows** button).

Tracing dependents

This shows the cells that depend upon the contents of the cell you have selected.

Ⓐ **Activity**

Select the cell **C7** and click the **Trace Dependents** button, the trace arrow will show those cells that depend upon the contents of **C7**, (i.e. those cells containing formulas which include **C7**).

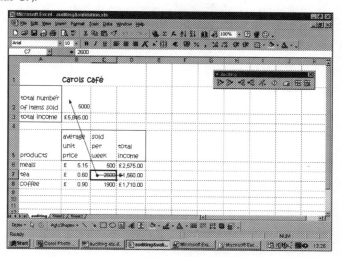

Remove the arrow by clicking the **Remove Dependents Arrows** button.

Tracing Errors

You can use this button to trace the cells making up a formula where the results are showing an error.

 Activity

Add the following text to cell **A10**:

average price per item

Use the **Format Painter** button to impose the same formatting as the other text cells.

In cell **B10,** enter the following formula:

=B3/C3

As this is not the correct formula and involves dividing a cell by zero, you will see an error message in the cell.

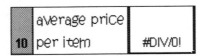

Select cell **B10** and click the **Trace Error** button, you will see trace arrows showing the cells making up the formula.

This should make it easier to correct the error.

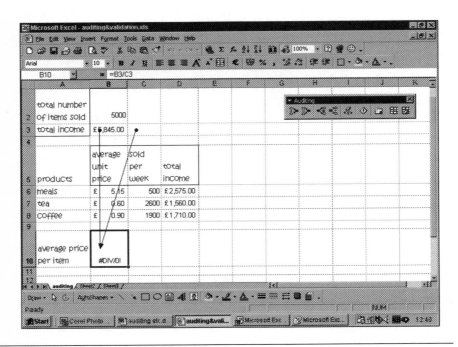

Use the **Remove All Arrows** button to remove the arrows.

Enter the correct formula into cell **B10**:

=B3/B2

Save and close the file.

Validating data

Excel enables you to set certain input values for a cell and to ensure that the data that is entered into that cell is between those values. It is also possible to create custom messages and comments for these cells.

Activity

Open the file **auditing & validation** and look at the worksheet **auditing.**

Select cell **B6**, pull down the **Data** menu and select **Validation**.

The **Data Validation** dialog box will be displayed.

Enter the following data into each of the boxes and then click the **Input Message** tab.

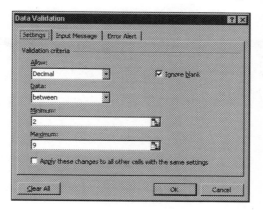

Enter the following text and then click the **Error Alert** tab.

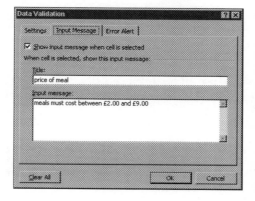

The **Error Alert** can be set to **Stop**, which refuses to accept any entry outside the range set, or **Warning**, which displays a warning but allows you to enter the data, or **Information**, which tells you that the entry is outside the range but allows it to be entered.

Enter the following text.

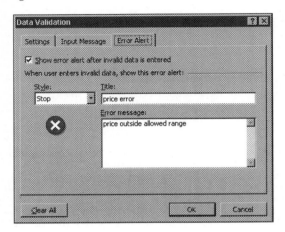

When you return to the worksheet and select cell **B6**, you will see that a message appears.

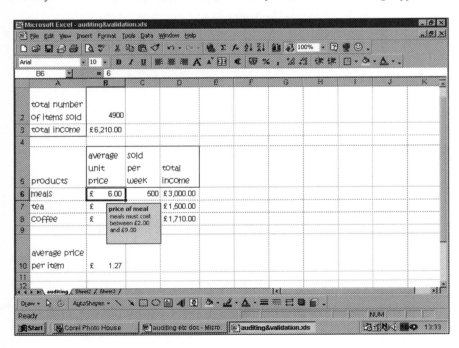

Now attempt to enter a figure outside the allowed range into cell **B6**.

An error message will appear and you will not be allowed to continue until you enter a figure within the allowed range of values.

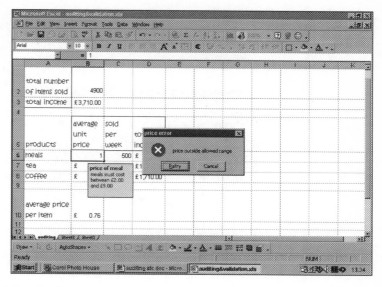

Save and close the file.

(E) Exercise

❑ Open a new workbook and save it as **fifth_example**.

❑ Enter the following data, using **AutoFormat** to format it.

A	B	C	D	E
Sales Forecast (first six months) 2000 (units)				
	birds	cats	dogs	frogs
jan	12	11	3	1
feb	11	12	5	2
mar	3	7	4	3
apr	5	9	7	5
may	9	8	6	2
jun	17	5	9	1

❑ Name this worksheet as **animals-sales**.

❑ Select cells **B3** to **B8**.

❑ Set up a validation rule (for these cells) so that the numbers entered must be **whole numbers** with a value between **0** and **10**.

❑ Set up suitable **Input Message** and **Error Alert** (but make this a **Warning** as opposed to a **Stop**).

❑ Check this by attempting to enter invalid data into any of the cells **B3** to **B8**.

❑ Save the file, retaining the original values.

Copying validation rules to existing data

You can copy any validation rules to other cells.

Activity

Select cell **B3**, click the **Copy** button, highlight the other cells (**B3** to **E8**) and then pull down the **Edit** menu, select **Paste Special**.

Select the **Validation** option and Click **OK**.

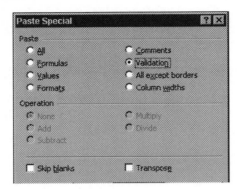

You should now have copied the validation rules to the other cells.

Circling Invalid Data

This auditing technique can be used in conjunction with the validation rules to circle data that is not within the set parameters.

 Activity

Display the **Auditing** toolbar and click the **Circle Invalid Data** button.

The cells containing data outside the allowed range will be circled in red.

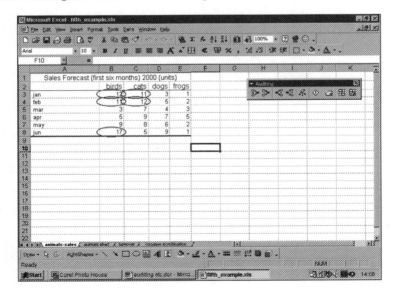

Remove the circles by using the **Clear Validation Circles** button.

Save and close the file.

Charting

Fun with Charts

This section looks at some of the variations of the normal charting options.

In this unit you will learn about:

- ❑ 3-D charts
- ❑ Doughnut charts
- ❑ Area charts
- ❑ Pictograms
- ❑ Combination charts
- ❑ Adding trendlines
- ❑ Creating a chart using data from two worksheets

3-D charts

 Activity

Open the file **first_example** and look at the worksheet **bonuses-chart**.

Create a copy of this chart (**Edit**, **Move or Copy Sheet**, remember to tick the **Create A Copy** box), move it to the end and rename it **bonuses-chart-3d**.

Pull down the **Chart** menu and select **Chart Type**.

Select the 7th choice (shown opposite) and the graph will change to look like this.

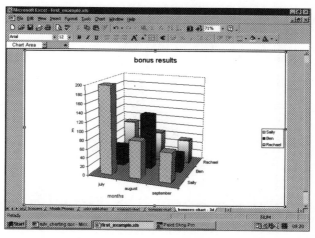

Altering the series order

You may want to change the order in which the series are displayed. This is often necessary when using **3-D column** charts so that all the columns are visible.

(A) *Activity*

Select any of the series and pull down the **Format** menu, select **Selected Data Series** and **Series Order**.

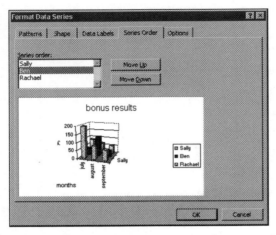

Use the **Move Up** and **Move Down** buttons to rearrange the series in the following order.

The chart should now look like this, the smaller columns in front of the larger.

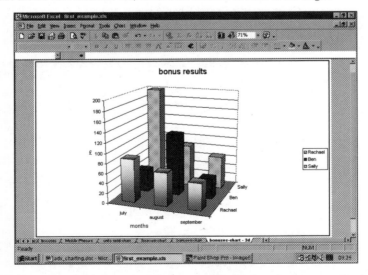

Sometimes it is not possible to arrange the series so that all the columns are easily visible.

Altering the 3-D view

With 3-D charts, it is possible to alter the angle at which you look at the data.

(A) *Activity*

Pull down the **Chart** menu and select **3-D View**.

Change the settings to those shown in the illustration below.

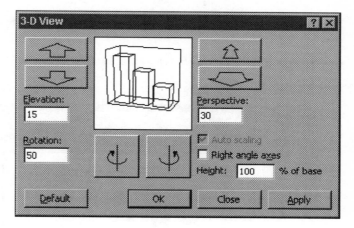

Add a border to the chart.

The chart should now look like this.

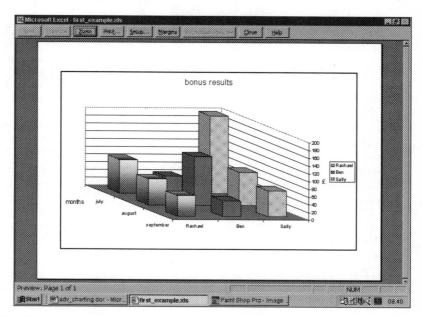

Adjust the settings to see the different effects you can achieve.

Save and close the file.

(E) *Exercise*

❑ Open the file **first_exercise** and look at the worksheet **costs2000**.

❑ On a new sheet create a **3-D column chart** from only the **Income** (**A3** to **D4**) and **Total Outgoings** rows (**A8** to **D8**), excluding the totals, adding titles and axis labels as necessary.

❑ Format the chart as you wish.

❑ Rearrange the series to show the columns to best advantage.

❑ Pull down the **Chart** menu, select **3-D View** and change the settings to show the chart to best effect.

❑ Give the worksheet the name **costs 2000-3D** and move it to the end.

The result may look similar to this.

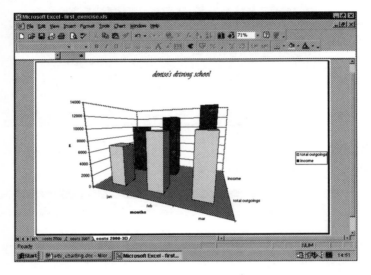

❑ Save and close the file.

Doughnut charts

This can be a very useful variation on the charting theme. Its importance is that it is similar to a **pie chart**, however you can chart more than one series within the chart, as opposed to a pie chart where only one series can be included in any one pie chart.

(A) *Activity*

Open the file **first_example** and look at the worksheet **bonuses**.

Highlight the data in cells **A2** to **D5** and begin the **Chart Wizard**.

In **Step 1**, select the first choice from **Doughnut**.

In **Step 3**, select the tab **Titles** and add the title:

Sales person/month

Also, in **Step 3**, select the **Data Labels** tab and choose **Show Percent**.

Finally, place the chart **As New Sheet**.

Rename the sheet as bonuses-doughnut and move it to the end.

At present it is not clear what each piece of the doughnut represents, so it would be useful to add arrows and text boxes to the chart (as shown in the next illustration).

To do this, you need to have the **Drawing** toolbar visible (if it is not, pull down the **View** menu, select **Toolbars**, followed by **Drawing**).

Select the **Text Box** tool, click and draw a box.

Enter the text, highlight the text and change the font, etc. as desired.

To draw an arrow, select the **Arrow** tool, click and drag to create the arrow. Double-click the arrow to format it as desired.

The text box and arrow can be dragged to a new position, sized and so on.

Use these techniques to add the text and arrows shown in the following illustration.

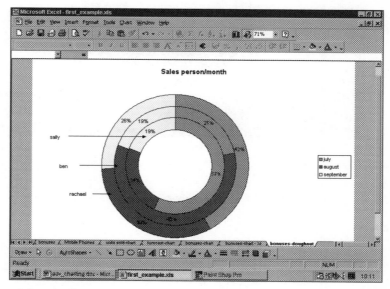

Save and close the file.

(T) Text boxes can be added to a worksheet containing data as well as to charts. In addition there are several other drawing tools available e.g. arrows, various shapes and symbols, etc.

(E) **Exercise**
- ❑ Open the file **second_exercise** and look at the worksheet **pamela's products**.
- ❑ Create a **doughnut** chart, on a new sheet, to show the **sales**, **purchases** and **total wages** for each of the three months, adding titles, etc. as necessary.
- ❑ Display the **labels** and **percentages** for each segment of the doughnut.

❑ Rename the sheet as **pam-doughnut** and move it to the end.

❑ Add arrows and text boxes to the chart to explain what each ring of the doughnut represents.

❑ Format the chart appropriately.

The result may look similar to this.

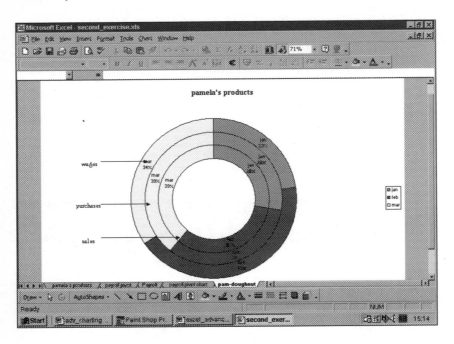

❑ Save and close the file.

Area charts

Another useful chart type is to plot the data in an **area chart**.

Activity

Open the file **first_example** and look at the worksheet **bonuses-chart**.

Create a copy of this chart (**Edit**, **Move or Copy Sheet**, remember to tick the **Create A Copy** box), move it to the end and rename it **bonuses-chart-area**.

Pull down the **Chart** menu and select **Chart Type**.

Choose **Area** charts and the 2nd of these.

The chart will change to an area chart and look like this (if the names are not shown in each of the areas, pull down the **Chart** menu, then select **Chart Options**, **Data Labels** and **Show label**).

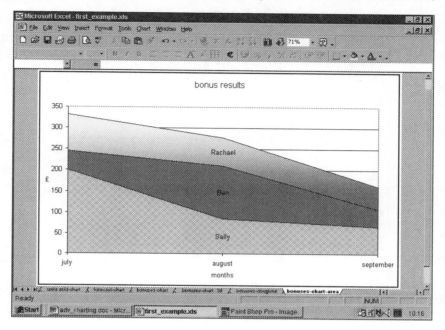

This type of chart is used to show totals over a period of time and the differing contributions to those totals.

Save and close the file.

Pictograms

Pictograms are a variation on column charts and involve the use of pictures to replace the original columns. They are often used in the popular press, as they are attractive and have immediate visual impact.

Ⓐ **Activity**

Open the file **fifth_example** and look at the worksheet **animals-sales**.

Create a column chart from the data in cells **A2** to **E8** (1st choice of column chart) and name this worksheet as **animals-chart** adding suitable titles and axis labels.

Switch back to the **animals-sales** worksheet and position the cursor in any blank cell.

Pull down the **Insert** menu, select **Picture** followed by **ClipArt**.

Select a picture of a **bird**.

Click the picture to select it and then click the **Insert Clip** button.

Select and cut the picture.

Switch back to the worksheet **animals-chart**.

Select the first series by clicking in one of the bars and making sure all the same colour bars have a small square in the middle to show they are selected.

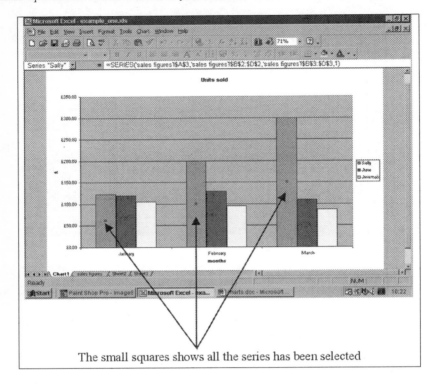

The small squares shows all the series has been selected

Click the **Paste** button to paste the image into the series.

Double-click the series (or pull down the **Format** menu followed by **Selected Data Series**), select the **Patterns** tab and click the **Fill Effects** button.

Click the **Stack and Scale to** option and then **OK** until you return to the chart.

The measurement in the **Stack and Scale to** box means there is one picture for every two units on the **Y-axis**. This can be changed to any measurement you wish.

The result should look like this.

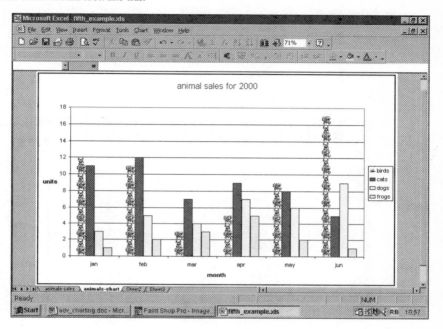

Apply the same technique to the other series in the chart, using suitable ClipArt images.

Finally, format the chart and you should see a chart similar to this.

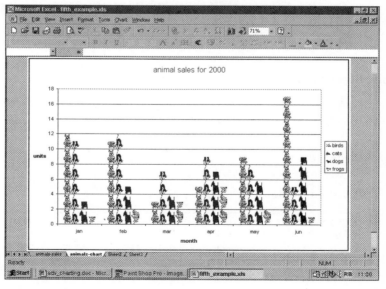

Save and close the file.

(E) **Exercise**

❑ Open the workbook **first_exercise**.

❑ Create a copy of the worksheet **costs 2000-3D** and name the new worksheet as **costs 2000-pictogram**.

❑ Alter the **Chart Type** to a column chart (1st choice of column chart).

❑ Insert **ClipArt** images into the chart to produce a pictogram and format the chart as desired including **stack and scaling**.

The result may look like this.

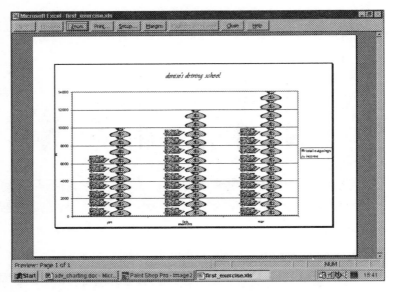

❑ Save and close the file.

Combination charts

A combination chart means a chart that contains more than one chart type, e.g. column and line. It is sometimes useful to superimpose a line on a column chart.

(A) **Activity**

Open the file **fifth_example** and look at *Sheet2*.

Add the following data.

Danny's Delly						
actual turnover v projected turnover for 2000						
	july	august	september	october	november	december
actual turnover (£)	1800	2600	2400	2500	1600	1800
projected turnover (£)	2000	2300	2400	2600	1900	1700

Rename the worksheet as **turnover**.

Create a **column chart** from the figures, adding suitable titles and axis labels.

Select the *second* series (projected turnover figures), pull down the **Chart** menu and select **Chart Type**.

Select **Line** from the list and you should now have a chart which shows the actual figures in columns and the projected figures as a line.

Rename the worksheet as **turnover-combination** and move it to the end.

Format the chart to your own satisfaction. The result should resemble the following illustration.

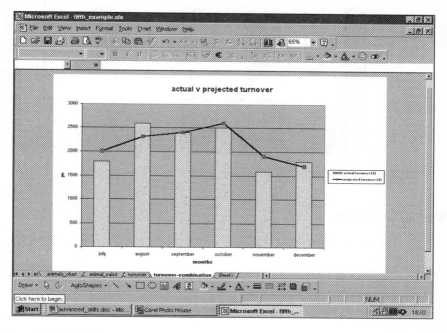

Save and close the file.

Ⓔ **Exercise**

❏ Open the workbook **first_exercise**.

❏ Create a copy of the worksheet **costs 2000-3D** and name the new worksheet as **costs 2000-combination**.

❏ Return to the worksheet **costs 2000** and (by copying and pasting) add the data for the **income less total expenses (A10 to D10)** to the chart **costs 2000-combination**.

❏ Change the **chart type** for the whole chart to a **column chart** (clustered column — 1st choice of column chart).

❏ Change the chart type for the series containing the **income less total expenses** into a line and format it so it is clearly visible.

❑ The result will look similar to this.

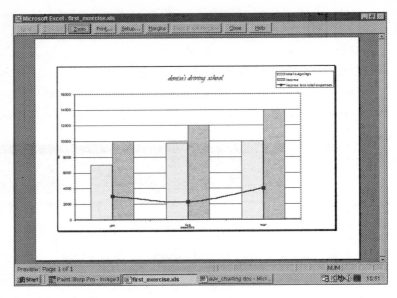

❑ Save and close the file.

Adding trendlines

You can add a trendline to a chart to show the trend or direction, e.g. to show if the overall trend of sales is upwards or downwards.

Ⓐ **Activity**

Open the file **fifth_example** and view the worksheet **turnover-combination**.

Pull down the **Chart** menu and select **Add Trendline**.

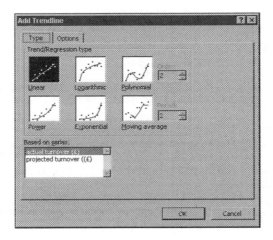

Select the options shown above and click the **OK** button; a trendline is added to the chart.

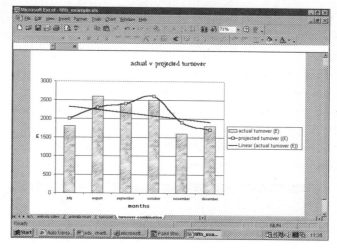

Save and close the file.

(E) *Exercise*

❑ Open the workbook **first_exercise**, look at the worksheet **costs 2000-combination**.

❑ Add a trendline to show the trend of the **income less total expenses**.

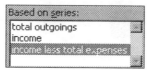

❑ The result will look similar to this.

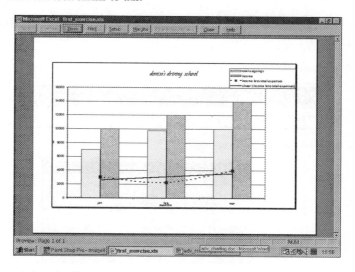

❑ Save and close the file.

Creating a chart using data from two worksheets

It is sometimes useful to be able to create a chart that uses data from two different worksheets, either within the same file or from different files.

 Activity

Open the file **first_exercise** (worksheet **costs 2000**).

Highlight the cells **A3 to D4** and the cells **A8** to **D8**.

Create a column chart (as a separate sheet) using this data, entering the titles, axis labels and formatting it as desired.

Rename the worksheet containing the chart as **comparison chart**.

The result should resemble the following illustration.

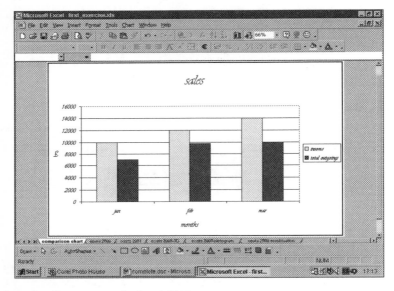

Pull down the **Chart** menu and select **Add Data**.

Use the mouse pointer, and **Ctrl** key, to select the following cells from the worksheet **costs 2001**.

You will then see another dialog box.

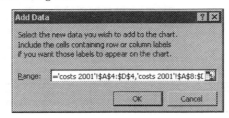

Click **OK**.

Finally, make sure the following choices are set in the next dialog box and click **OK**.

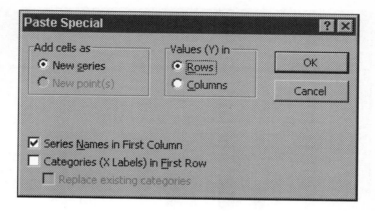

The new series will be added to the chart, format the series so that it is easy to distinguish between the different series.

It may also be necessary to change the series labels in the **legend** to distinguish between the income and outgoings for each year.

To do this, pull down the **Chart** menu, select **Source Data** followed by **Series**.

Alter the names of each of the series to that shown below, by clicking the **Series** and then clicking in the **Name** box and typing the new name.

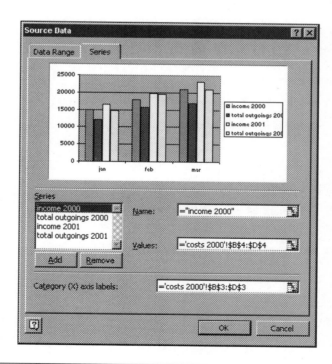

The result should look similar to this.

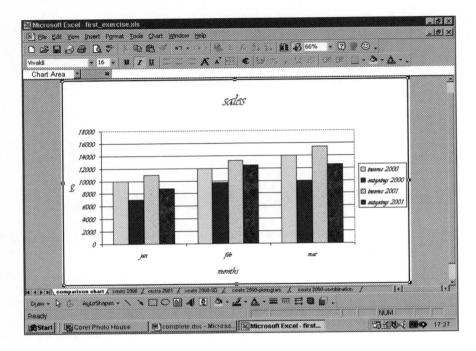

Save and close the file.

Using Excel to create web pages

In this unit you will learn:

❑ How to create web pages from your Excel workbooks

❑ How to add hyperlinks to Excel workbooks

Creating web pages

With the rapidly increasing importance of both the Internet and company Intranets, web functionality has been added to Microsoft® applications.

Excel can be used to create web pages.

 Activity

Open the file **first_exercise** and make sure that you are looking at the worksheet **costs 2000**.

Pull down the **File** menu and select **Save as Web Page**.

You will see the following dialog box.

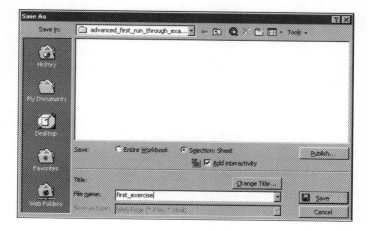

Change the settings to those shown above (**Selection:Sheet**, **Add interactivity**) and click the **Publish** button.

Accept the settings on the next dialog box (ensure that the **Sheet All contents of costs 2000** is highlighted).

Depending upon the setting you may need to tick the **Open published web page in browser** option.

Finally, click the **Publish** button

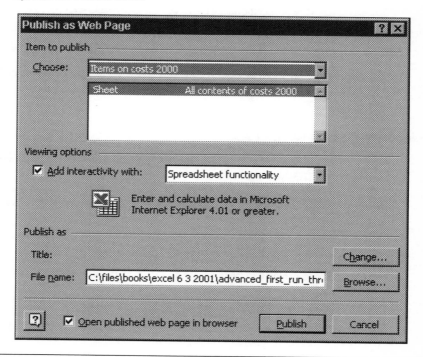

The page will be saved and **Microsoft Internet Explorer** (or your default browser) will open with the page displayed.

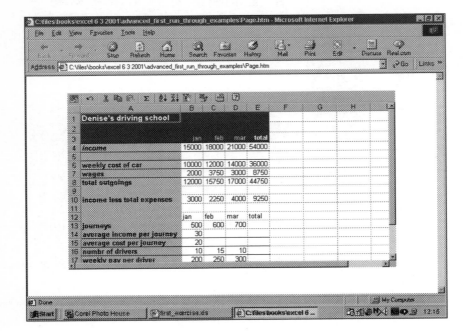

When accepting the choices in the dialog boxes you chose to enable **interactivity**, this means that the viewer can change the data and see the result within the displayed web page.

The page you have created can be added to a web site.

Close down **Microsoft Internet Explorer** and close the Excel file, saving any changes.

Adding hyperlinks to worksheets

Much of web functionality is based upon the use of **hyperlinks** (the ability to move from one page to another or from one web site to another).

You can add hyperlinks to your Excel pages, both to web pages **and** normal Excel worksheets.

 Activity

Open the workbook **projections**, you are going to add hyperlinks so that you can move between workbooks easily.

In the worksheet **solving** add the following text to cell **A10**:

Go to auditing & validation workbook

Place a border around the cell.

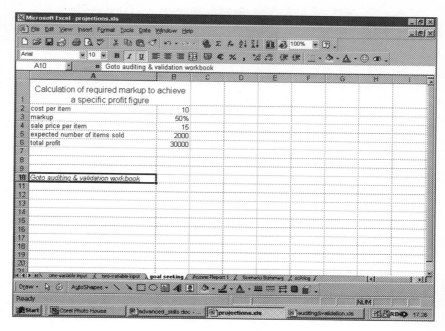

Right-click the text and select **Hyperlink** from the menu.

A dialog box will be displayed.

Use the *Browse for:* **File** button to find the workbook **auditing&validation** and click **OK**.

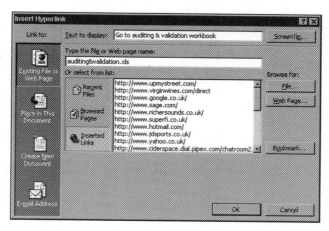

Click the **OK** button and the text should now be a hyperlink.

Move the mouse pointer onto the text and the pointer will change to a hand.

At this point, you activate the hyperlink by clicking it.

The file **auditing&validation** is opened automatically.

Ⓔ **Exercise**

❏ In cell **E1** of the workbook **auditing&validation** (worksheet **auditing**), enter the following text:

Go to the projections workbook

❏ Make this into a hyperlink (to the **projections** workbook) and then click it to see if it works.

❏ If your hyperlinks work, you should be able to click either to move to the other workbook.

❏ Save and close all the open files.

Working with Excel

Customising the toolbars
You can add or remove buttons from any visible toolbar so that the toolbar will contain the commands you use most often.

Adding buttons
To do so, pull down the **Tools** menu, click the **Customize** option and then **Commands**.

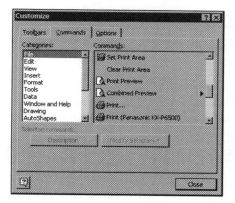

Select from the **Categories** list, followed by the **Commands** you want to add to a toolbar. Click and drag the buttons onto any of the visible toolbars.

Removing buttons
You can remove buttons by clicking and dragging the button off the toolbar (the **Customize** dialog box needs to be open to do this).

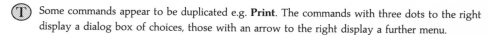 Some commands appear to be duplicated e.g. **Print**. The commands with three dots to the right display a dialog box of choices, those with an arrow to the right display a further menu.

Zooming the view
You can change the number of cells visible within a window by using the **Zoom** feature.

Increasing the zoom figure makes the data (or chart) larger but you see less cells, decrease the figure and you will see more cells but the contents of each will be smaller.

There are two methods of zooming:

❑ Use the **Zoom** command within the **View** menu, this is the most precise as you can enter any figure in the **Custom** box.

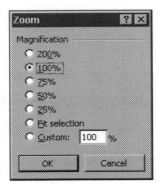

❑ Use the **Zoom** button on the **Standard** toolbar.

Full screen view

You can view the worksheet area without the various toolbars cluttering the screen by pulling down the **View** menu and selecting **Full Screen**.

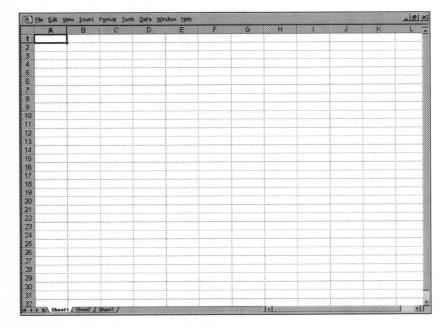

To revert to displaying the toolbars, repeat the procedure.

Displaying gridlines

Gridlines are shown on the worksheet by default and it is unlikely that you would want to remove them.

However, if you do then pull down the **Tools** menu and select **Options**. Click the **View** tab and remove the tick to the left of the word **Gridlines** (by clicking the box containing the tick).

To view the gridlines again, replace the tick.

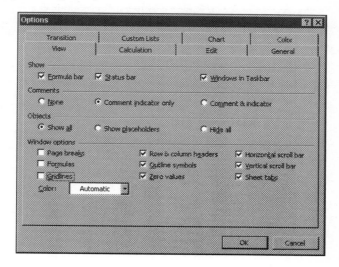

Printing gridlines

If you want to print the gridlines (Excel normally defaults to not printing them), then pull down the **File** menu, select **Page Setup** followed by **Sheet**.

Click the option **Gridlines** so that it has a tick and the gridlines will appear on the printout.

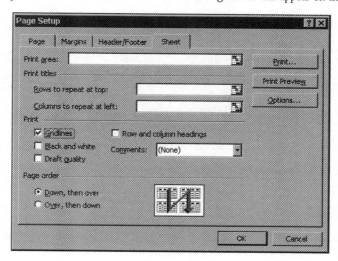

Highlighting rows or columns

❏ You can highlight individual rows or columns by clicking the mouse pointer on the row number or column letter.

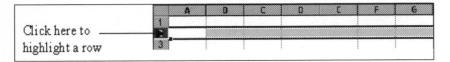

❏ To select more than one row or column click and drag the mouse, beginning with the first row number or column letter that you want to select.

❏ To select non-sequential rows or columns, highlight the initial rows or columns and then hold down the **Ctrl** key while clicking the mouse on the other row numbers or column letters.

❏ To highlight the whole worksheet, click the mouse in the top left corner of the worksheet where the rows and columns meet.

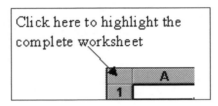

AutoSave

Excel defaults to **AutoSaving** your file every 10 minutes and a prompt will appear onscreen to remind you that this is taking place.

You can alter the time between **AutoSaves** or remove this feature.

To do so, pull down the **Tools** menu, select **AutoSave** and the dialog box will appear.

Make any changes and click the **OK** button.

AutoCalculate

Excel automatically recalculates whenever you change the numeric data within a worksheet. This can (with very large worksheets and old processors) slow down your work.

To change this setting, pull down the **Tools** menu, select **Options** and then **Calculation**.

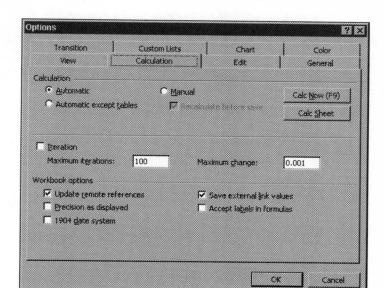

Change the settings (note that the **F9** key can be used to recalculate if you have turned off the AutoCalculate feature).

Decimal places

❑ You can select whether you want the decimal point to be automatically entered or whether you wish to enter it manually.

❑ The default is normally for Excel to assume that the figure you enter has two decimal places.

❑ If you **do not** want Excel to automatically enter the decimal point then pull down the **Tools** menu, select **Options**, followed by **Edit**.

❑ Remove the tick from the **Fixed decimal** box and then when you enter figures they will be entered as whole numbers. If you subsequently want to include decimal places, you will need to enter the decimal point manually.

AutoCorrect

Excel contains a feature called **AutoCorrect**. This automatically replaces some words you have typed incorrectly with the correct word.

To make changes to the settings or to add words (or phrases), pull down the **Tools** menu and select **AutoCorrect**.

Enter the desired text in the **Replace** and **With** boxes.

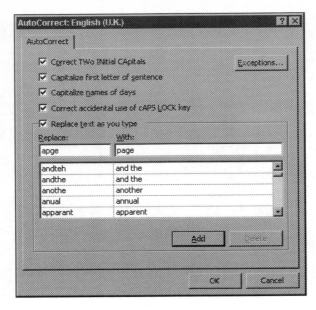

If you find the feature irritating, you can turn it off by clearing the tick from the **Replace text as you type** box.

AutoComplete

This feature completes the data you are entering based upon data you previously entered into the worksheet.

If you want to remove this feature so that Excel does not second guess the data you intend to enter, pull down the **Tools** menu, select **Options** and click the **Edit** tab.

Remove the tick from the **Enable AutoComplete for cell values** box.

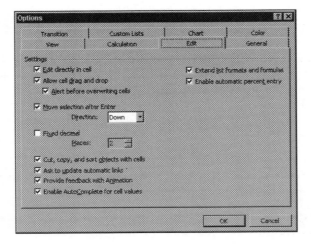

Shortcut keys

There are various shortcut key s which can be used to speed up your work.

Here is a selection that may be useful to you.

Select the current column	CTRL + SPACEBAR
Select the current row	SHIFT + SPACEBAR
Move to the beginning of the worksheet	CTRL + HOME
Move to the last cell on the worksheet	CTRL + END
Select all (when you are not entering or editing a formula)	CTRL + A
Calculate all sheets in all open workbooks	F9
Enter the date	CTRL + ; (semicolon)
Enter the time	CTRL + : (colon)
Display the Format Cells dialog box	CTRL + 1
Cut	CTRL + X
Copy	CTRL + C
Paste	CTRL + V
Undo	CTRL + Z
Save	CTRL + S
Print	CTRL + P
Open	CTRL + O
Insert a new worksheet	SHIFT + F11
Display the Find dialog box	SHIFT + F5
Repeat the last Find action (same as Find Next)	SHIFT + F4

Index